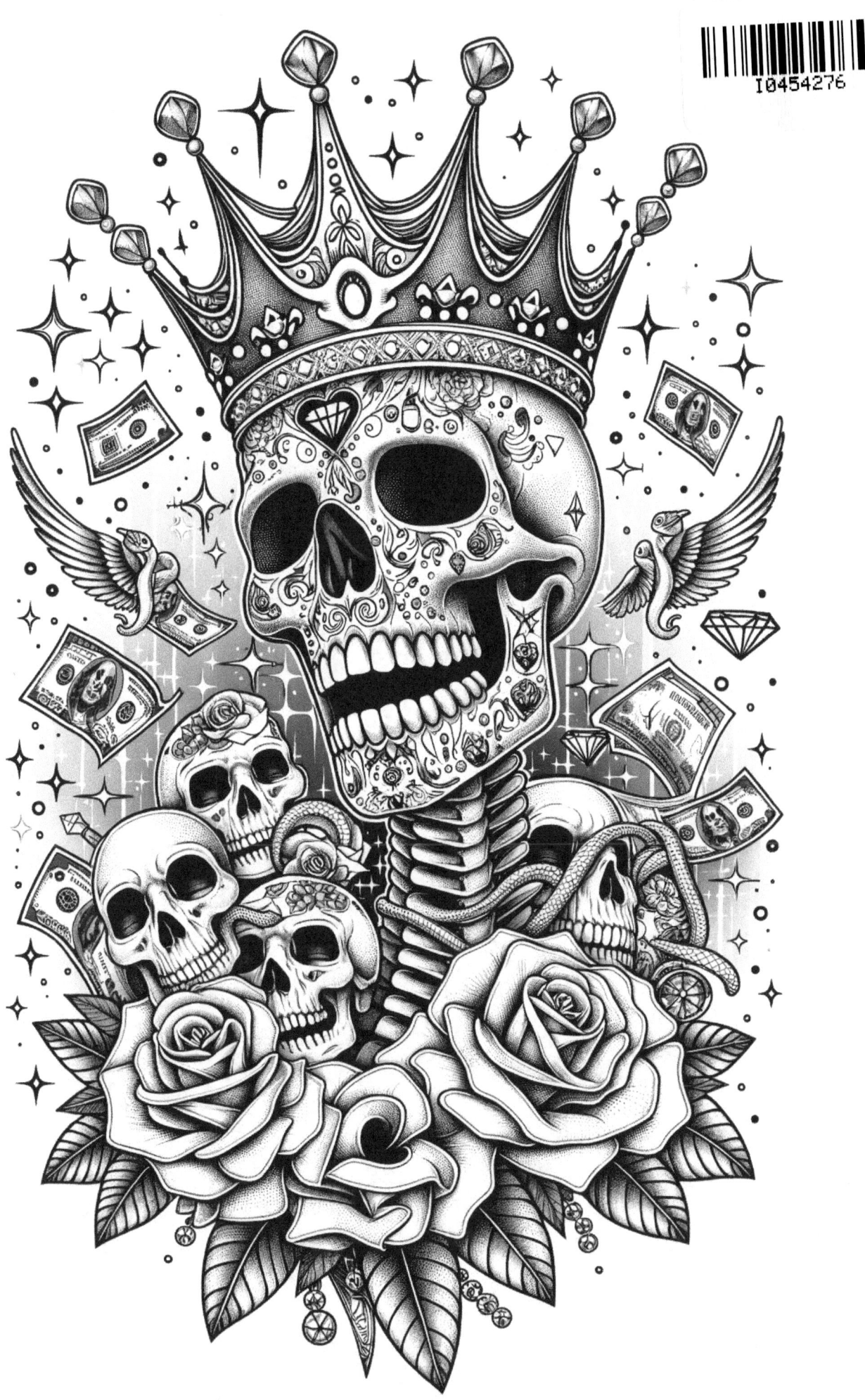

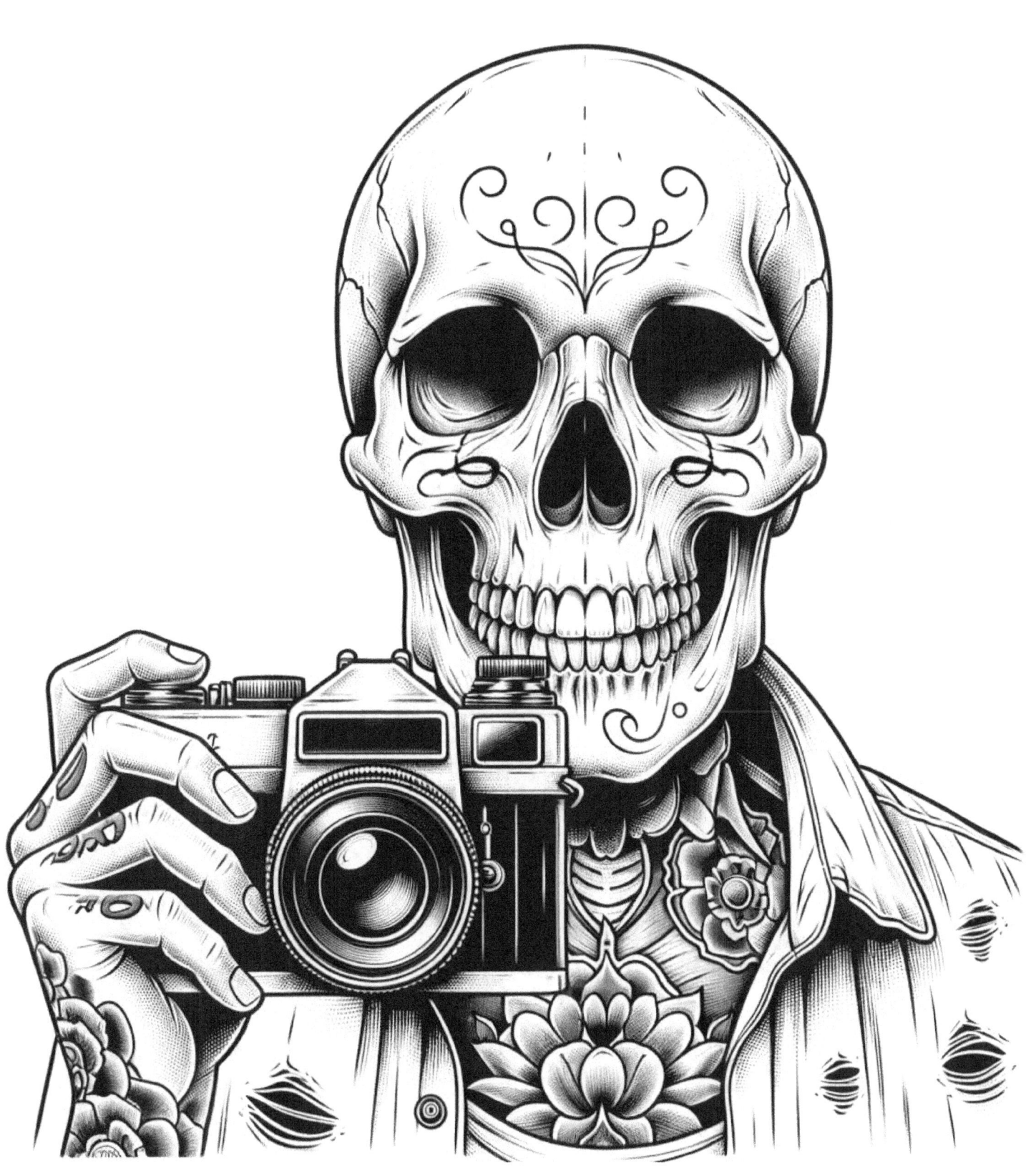

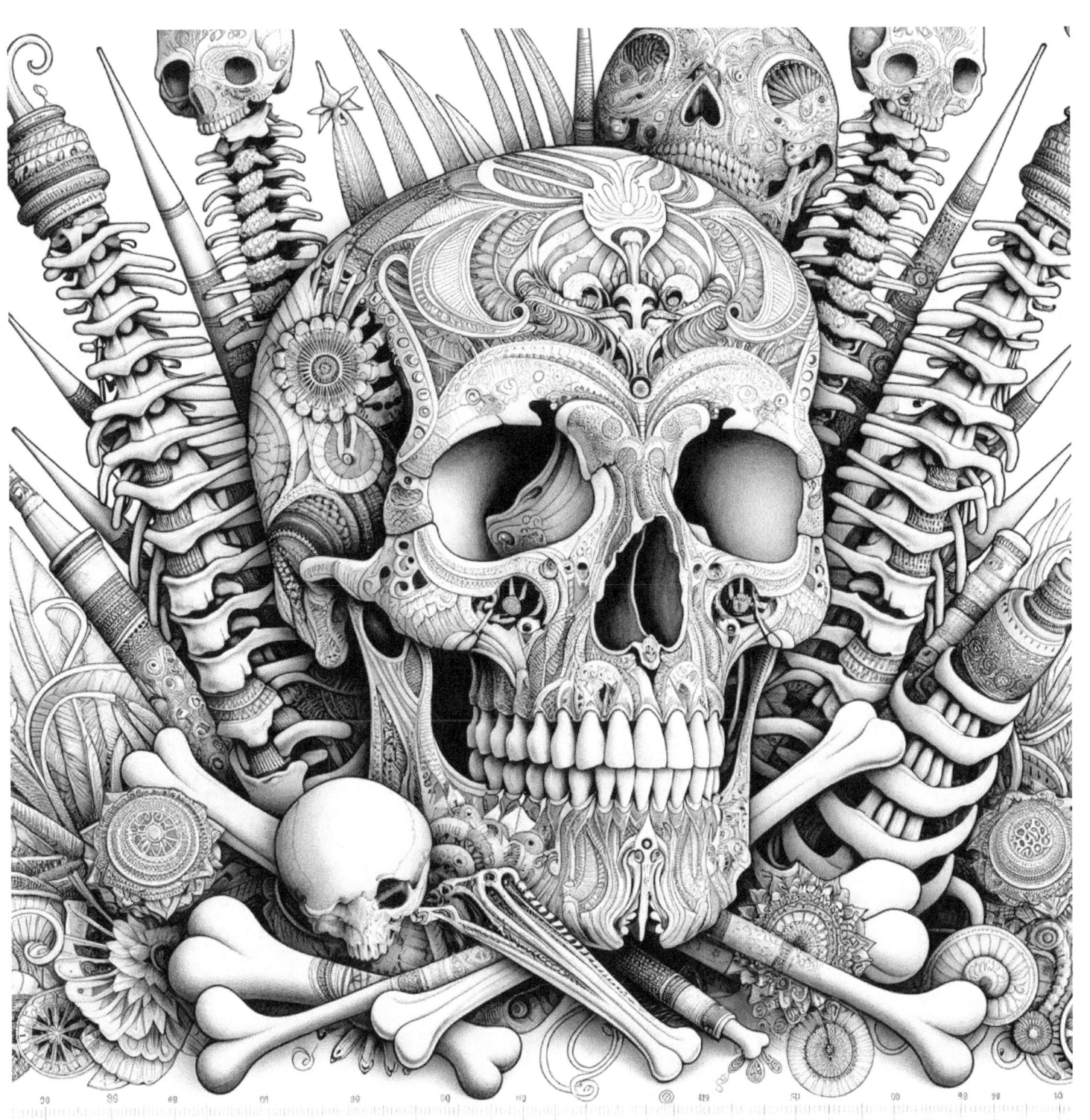

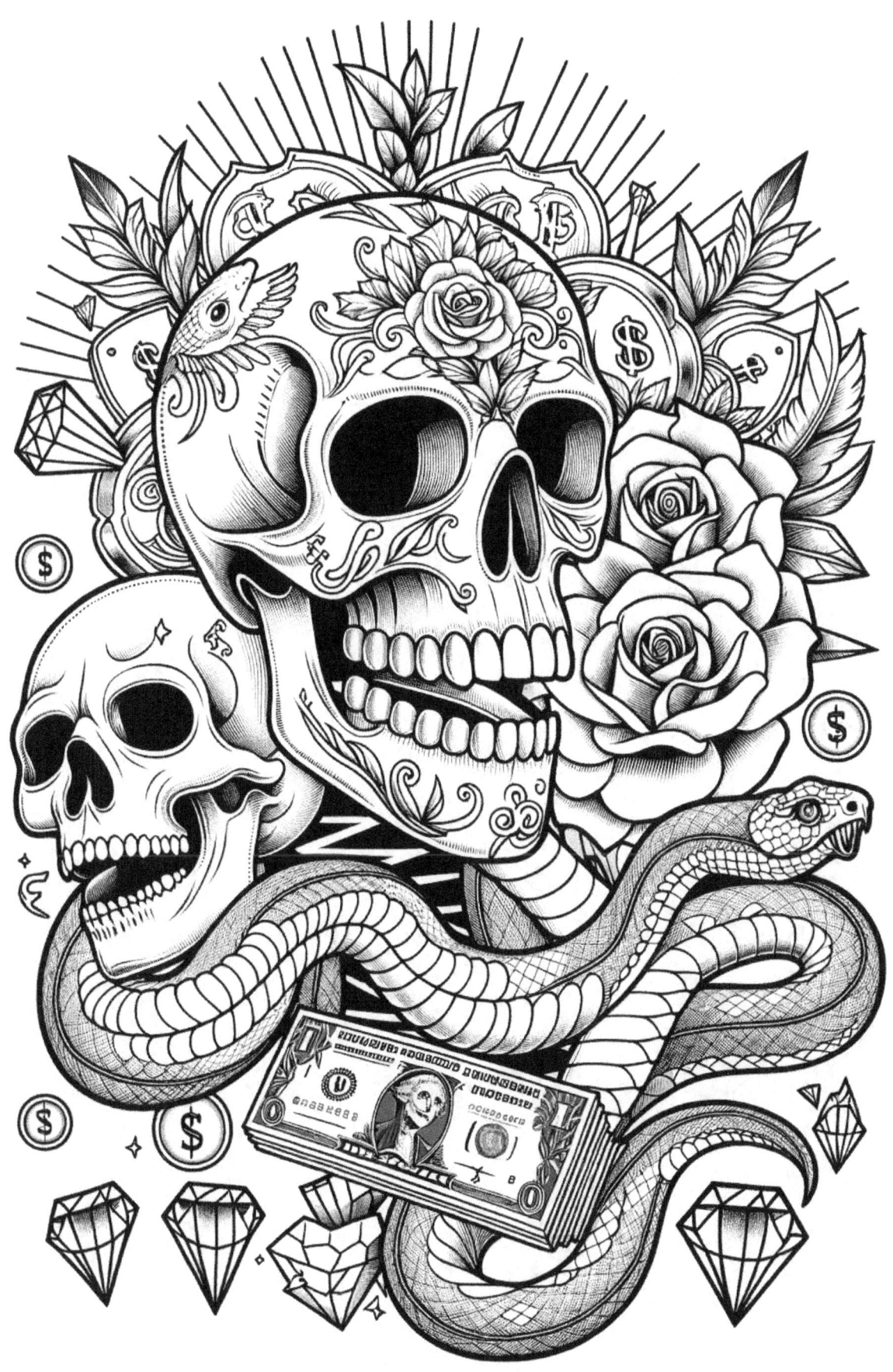

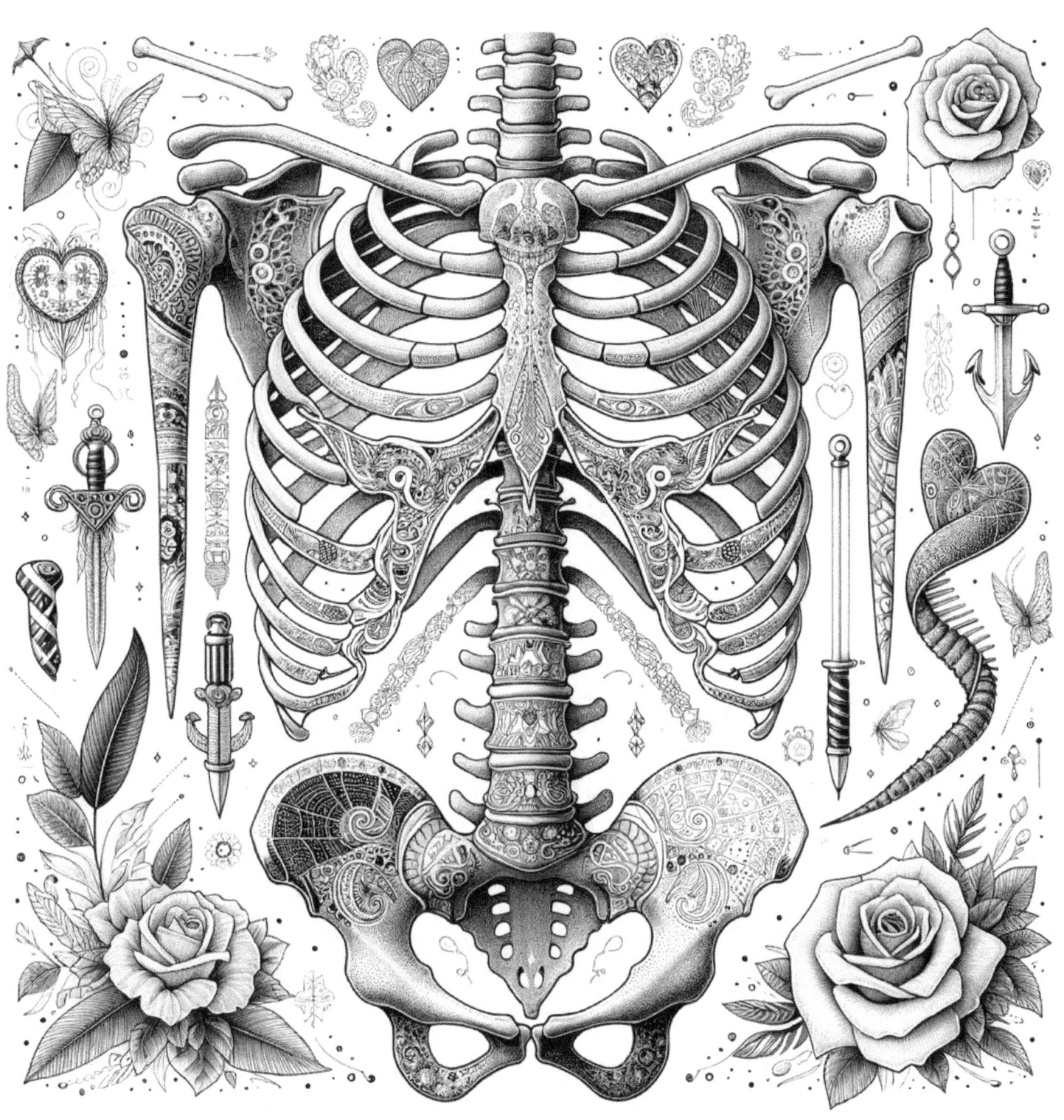

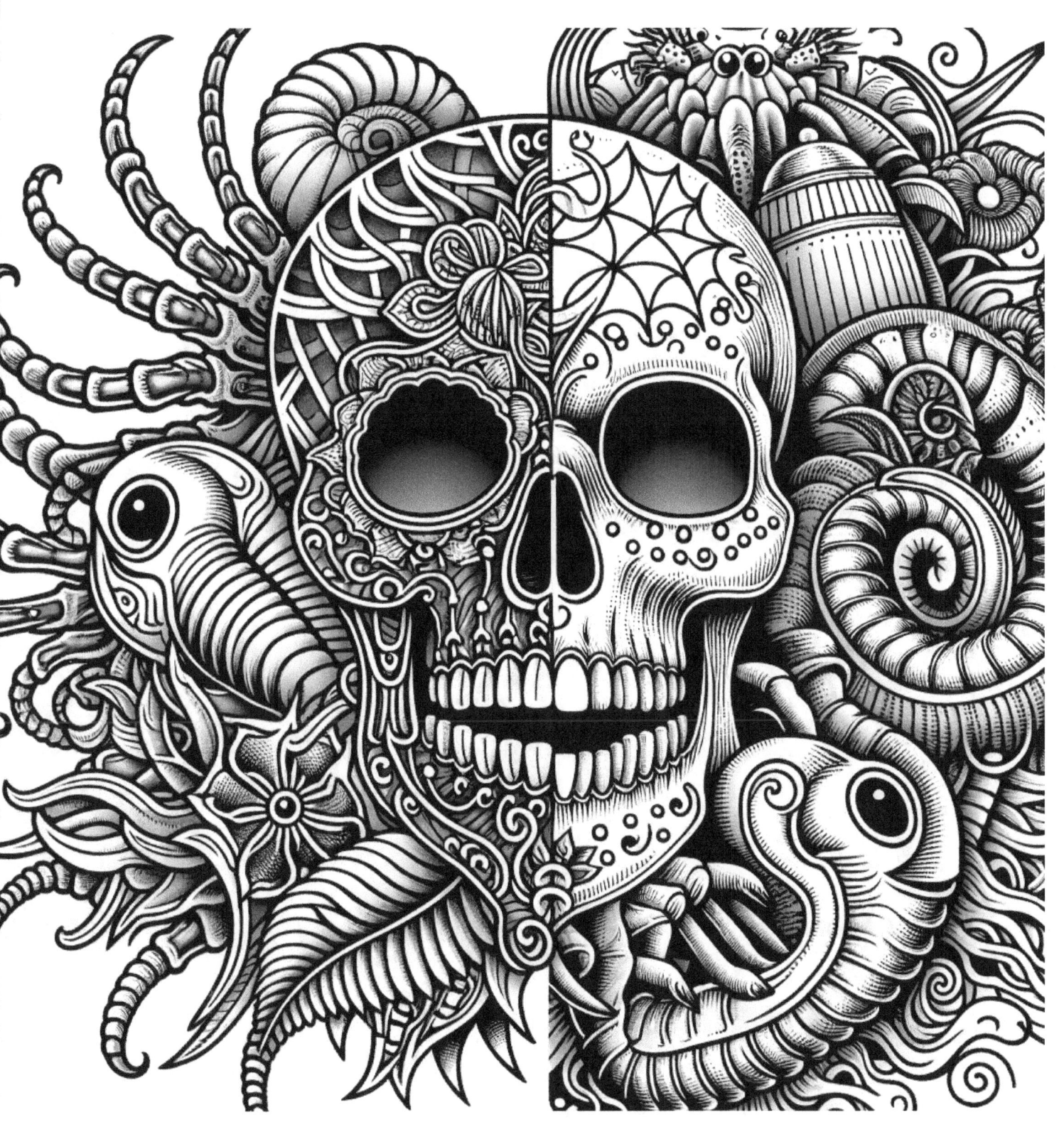

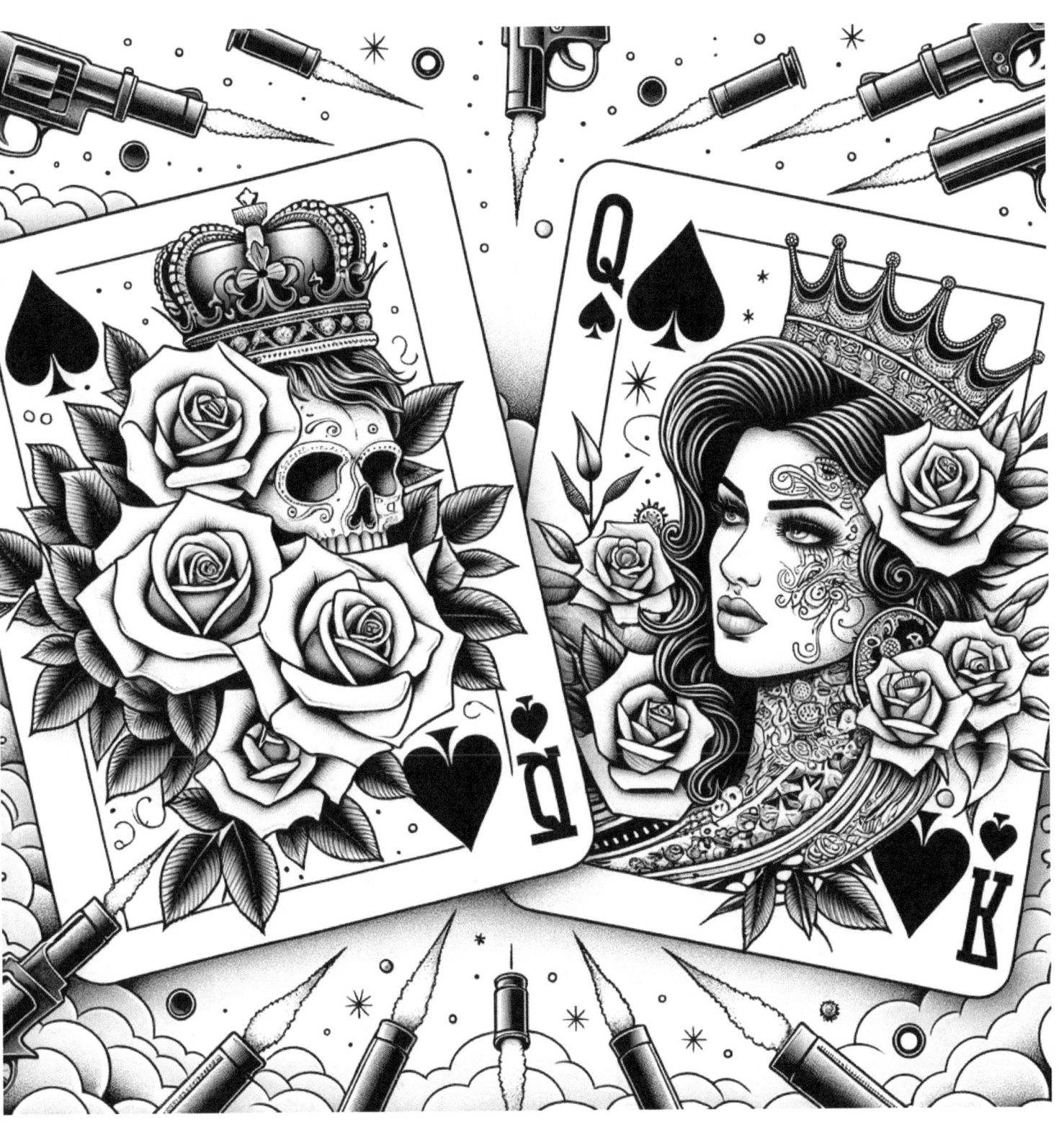

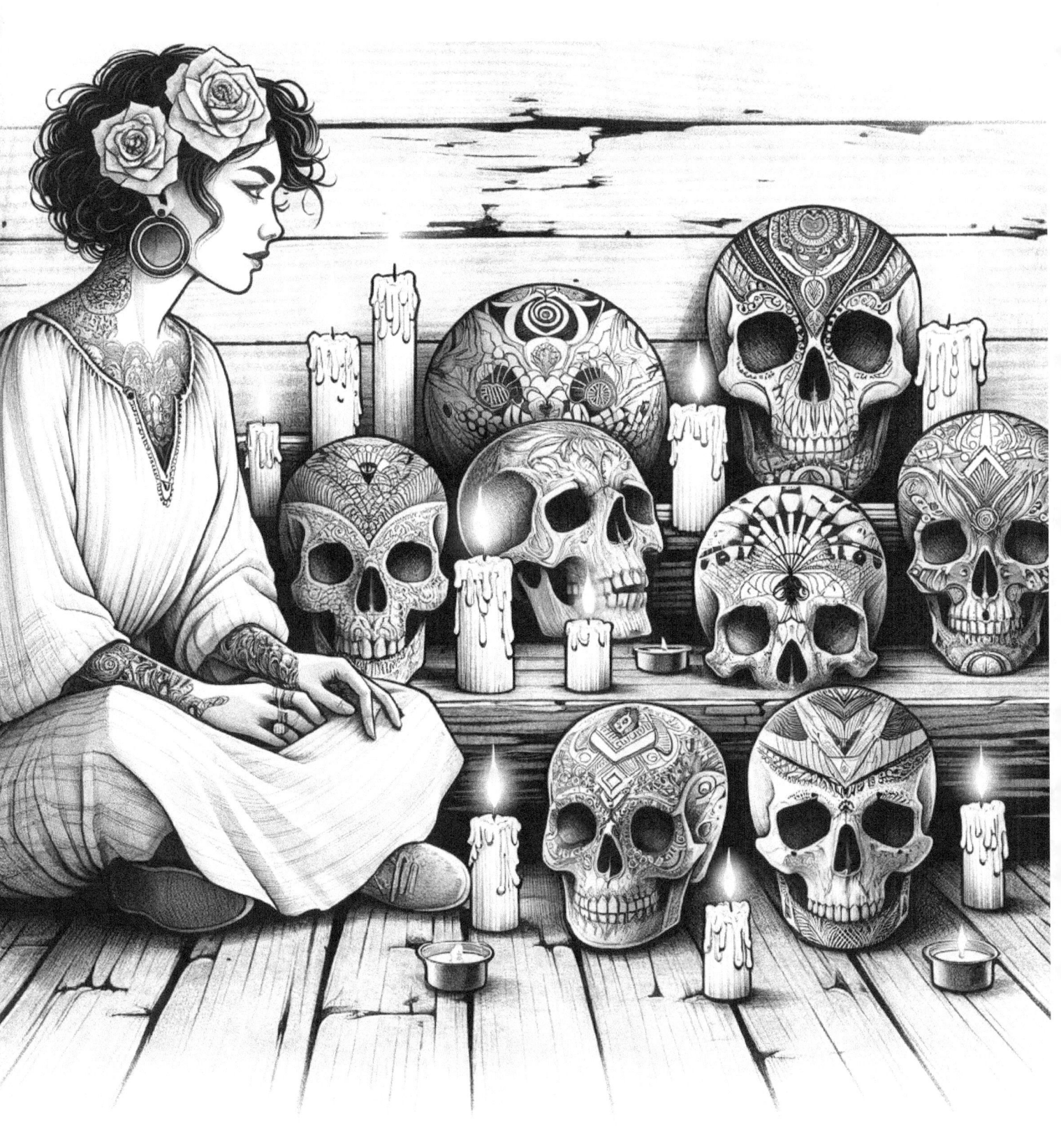

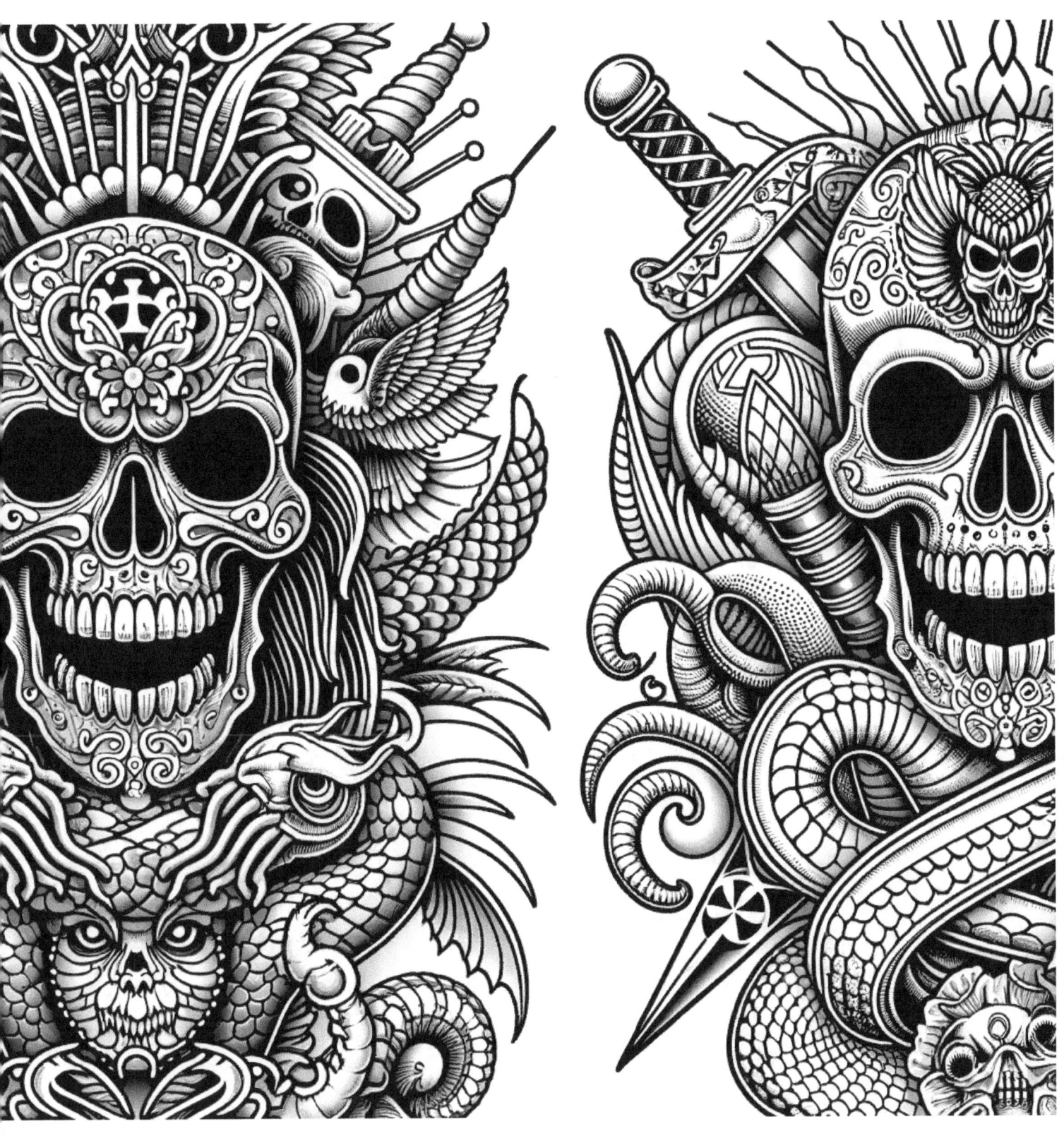

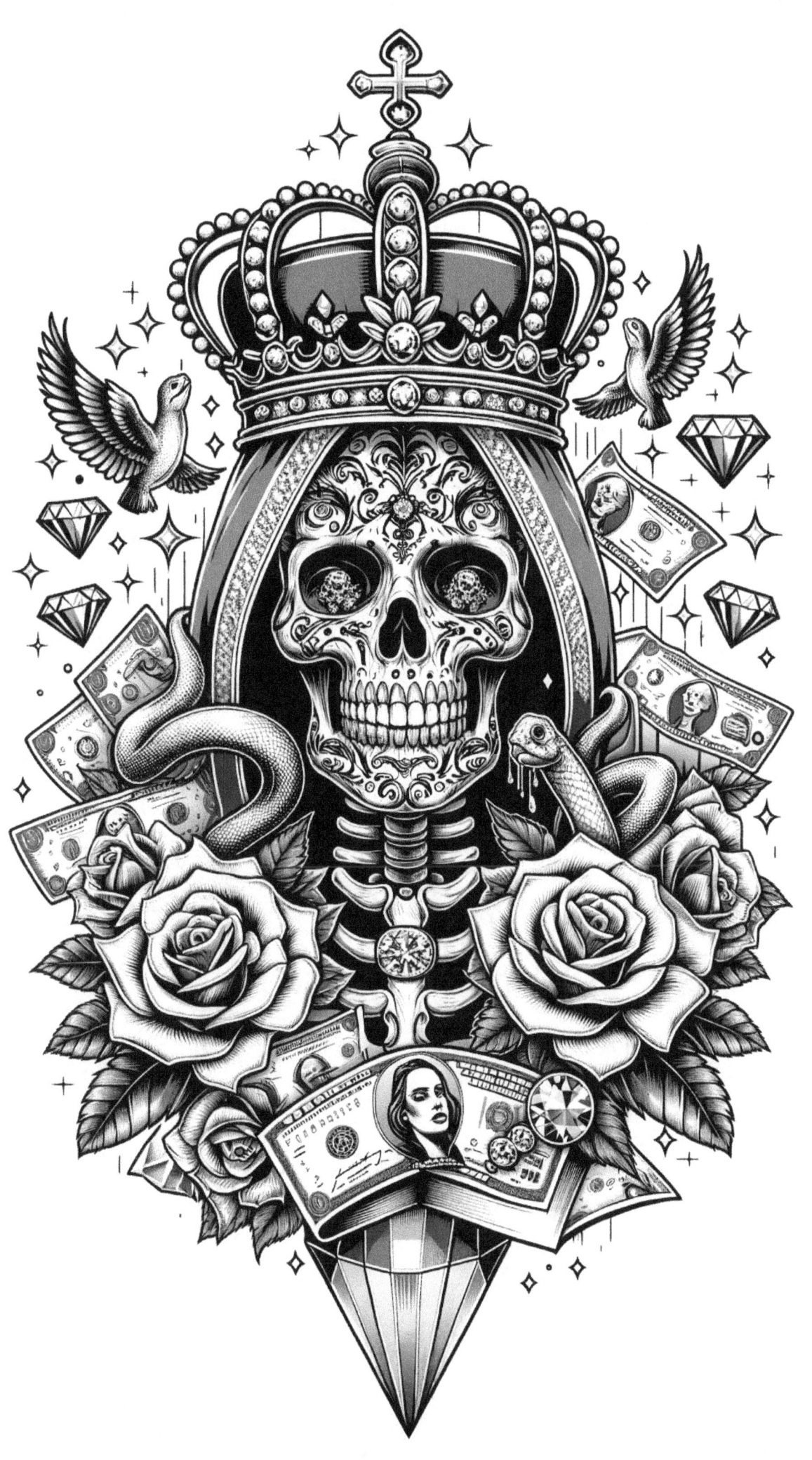

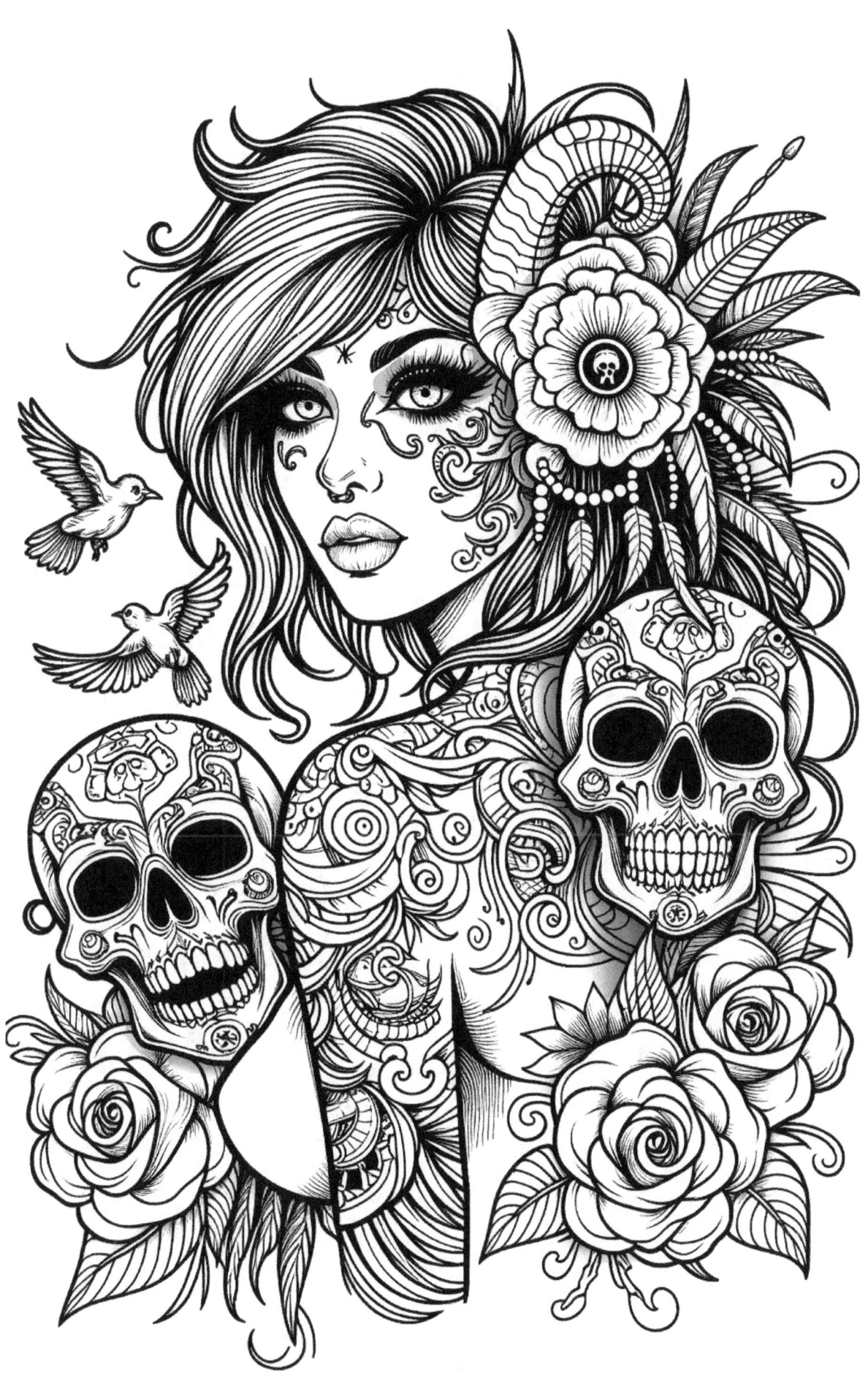

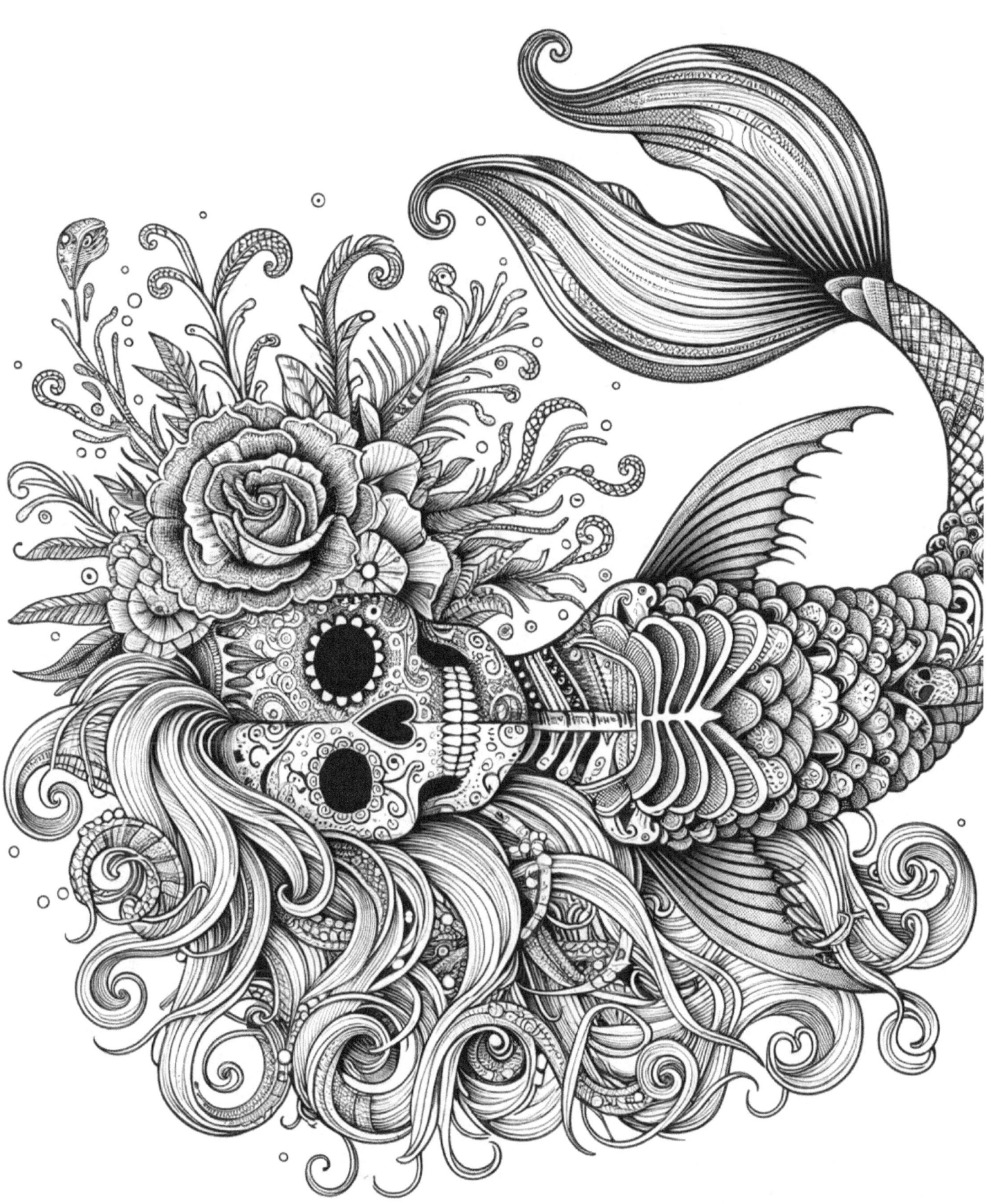

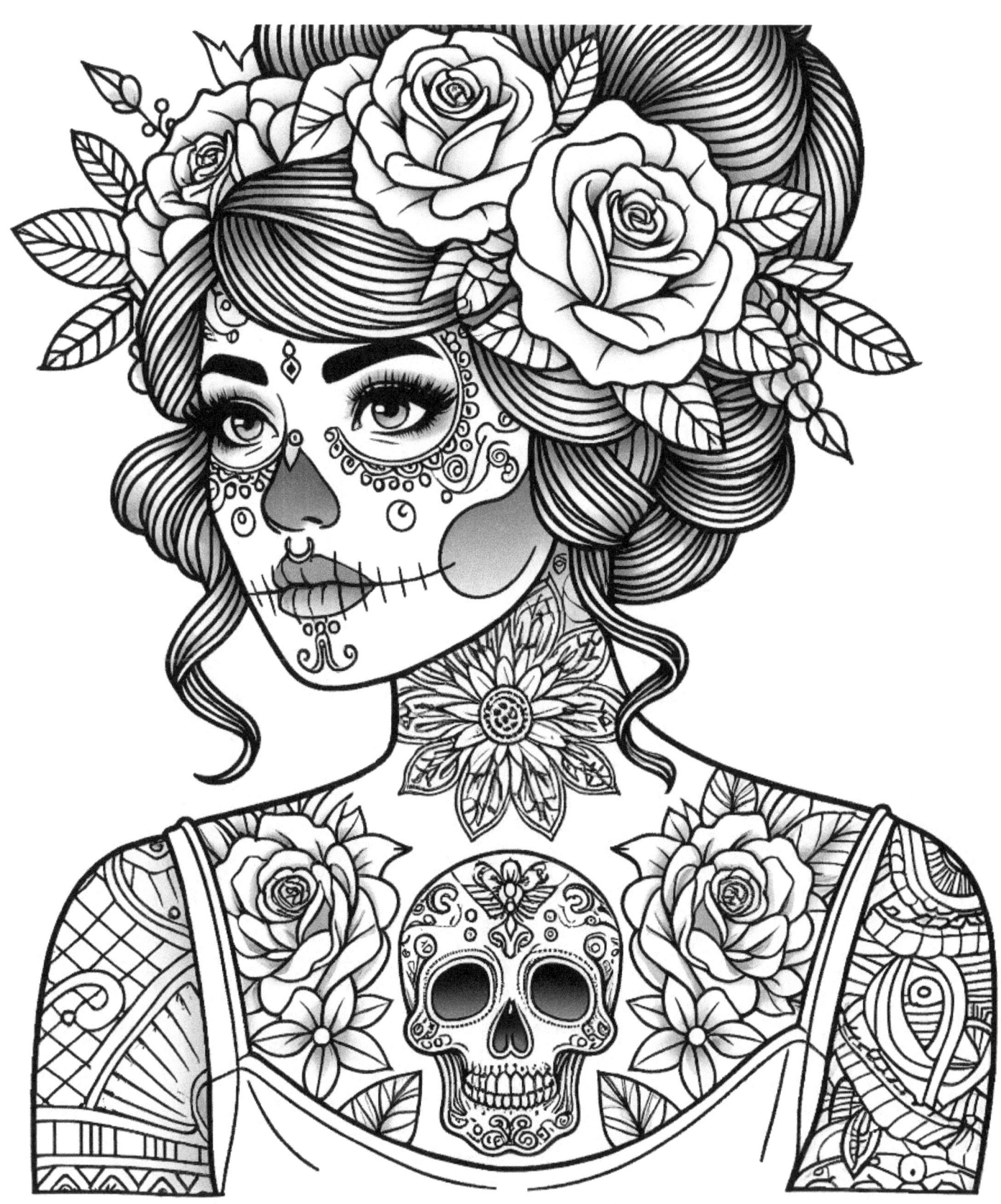

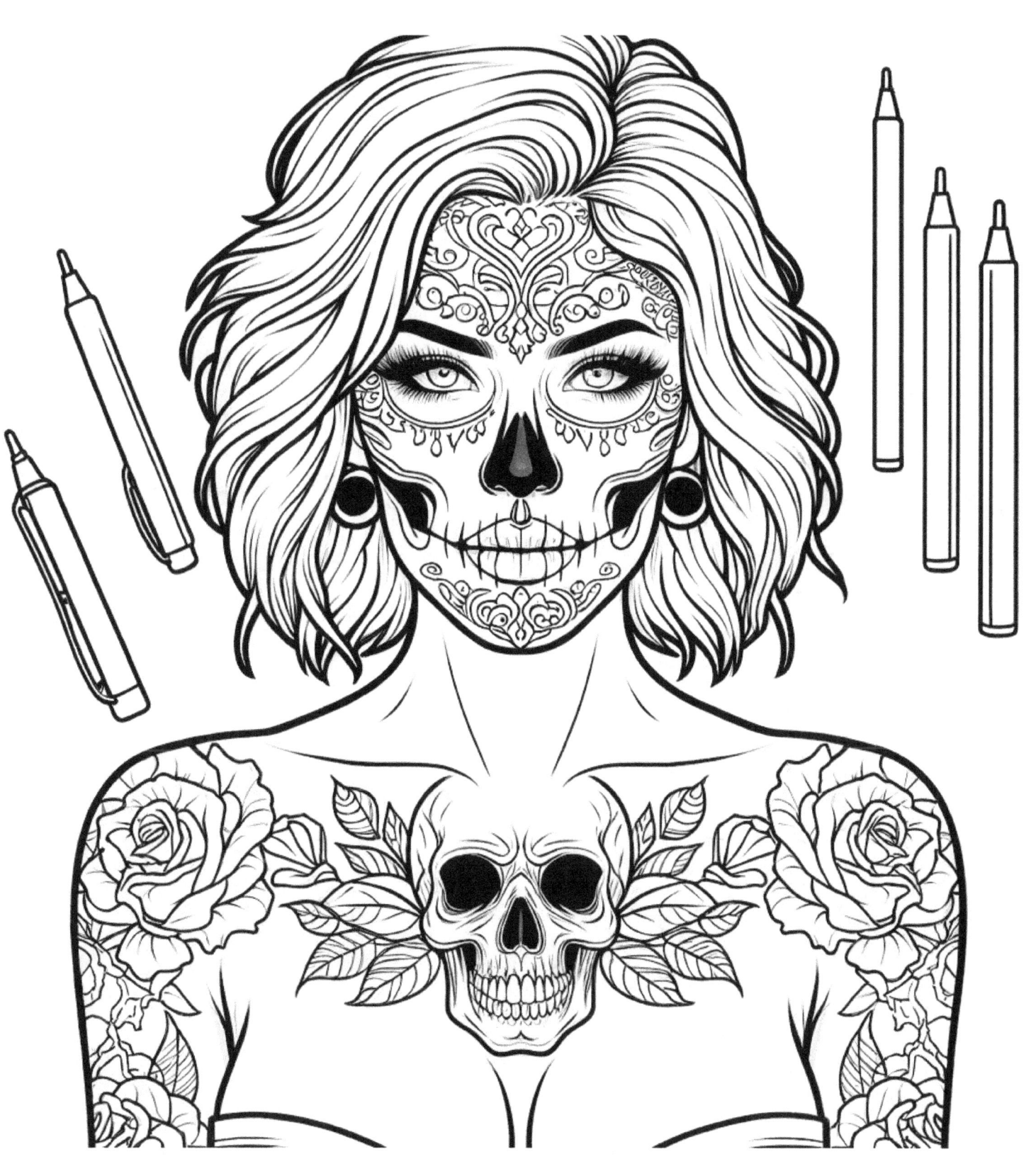

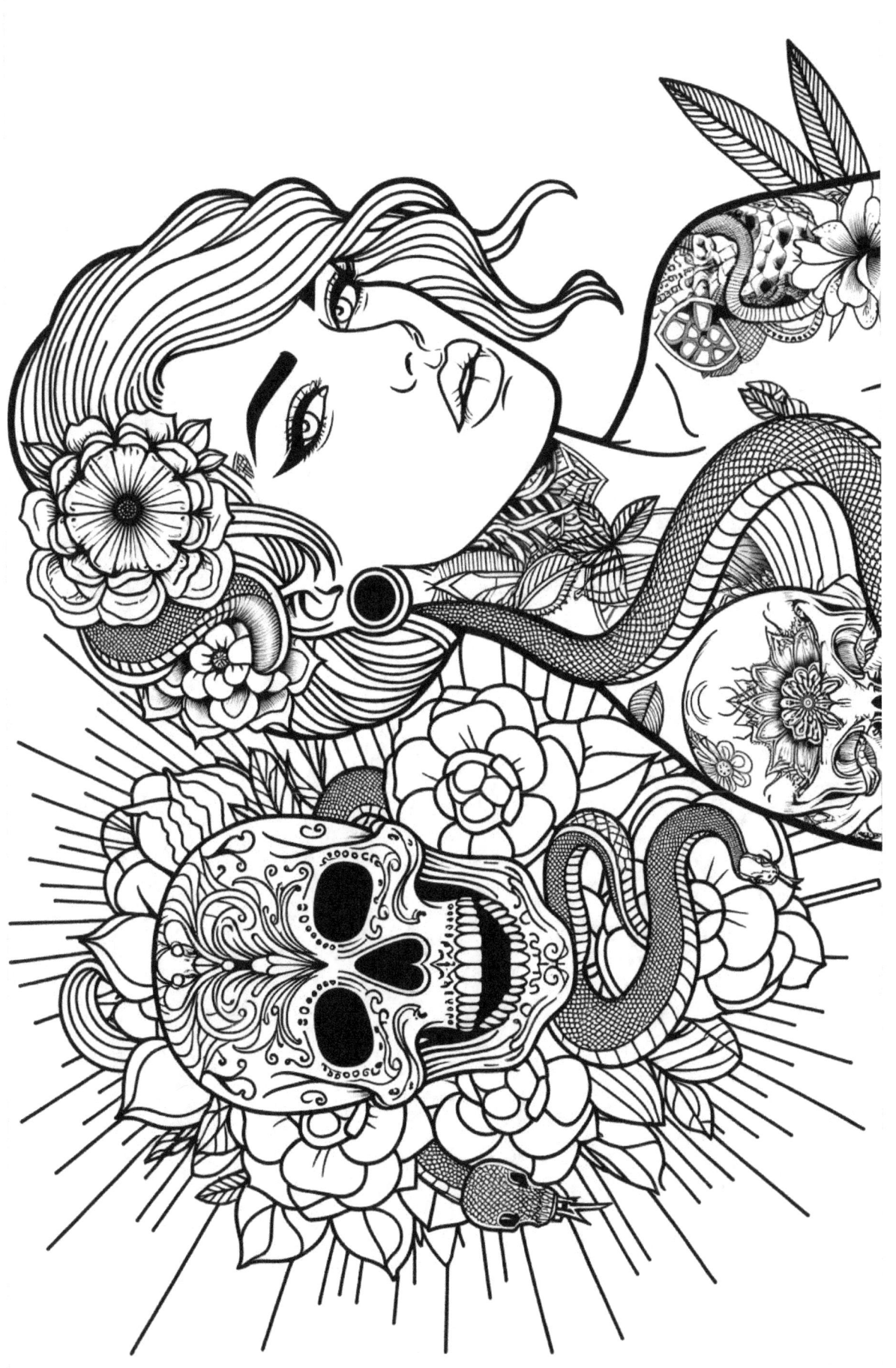

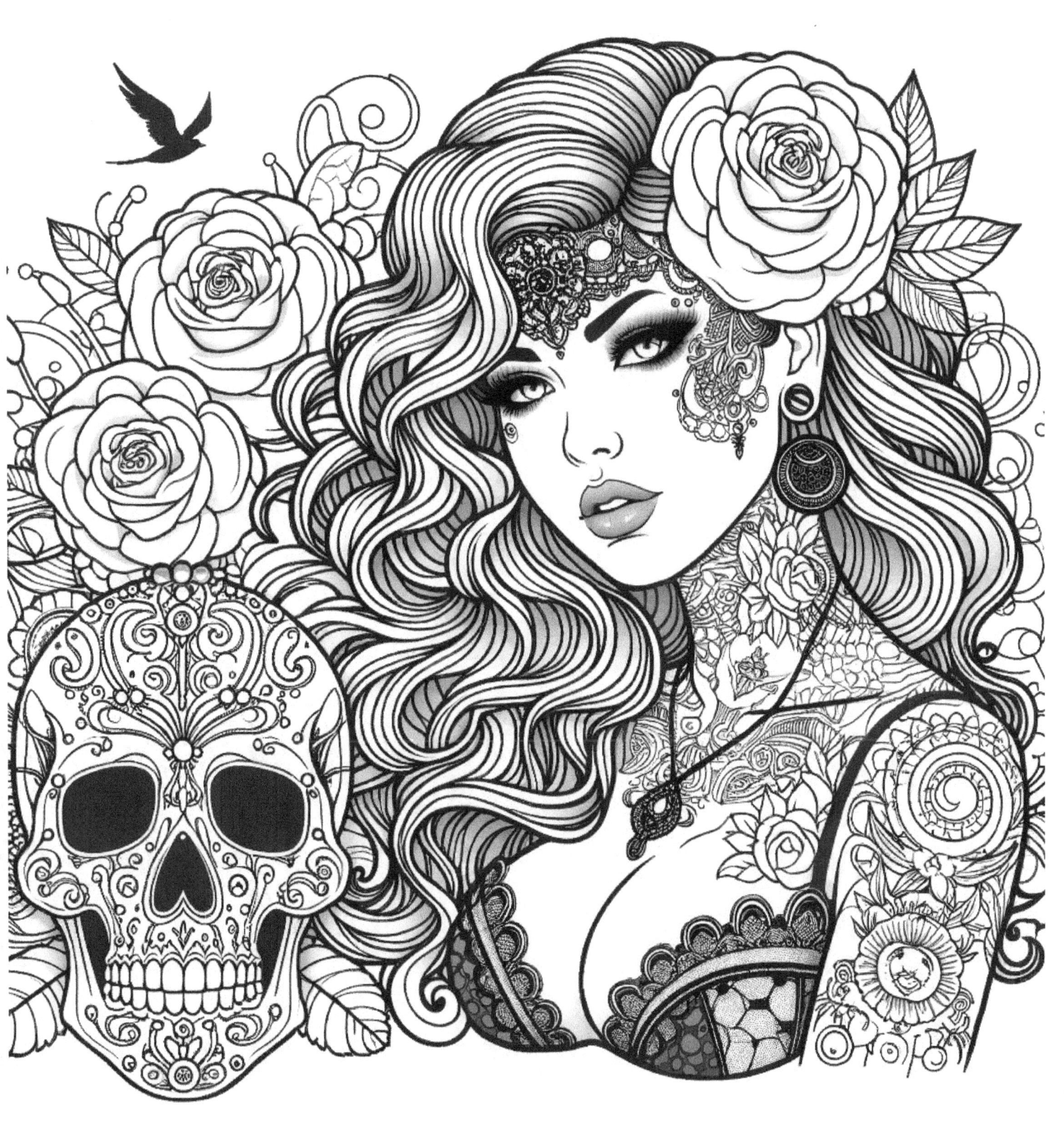

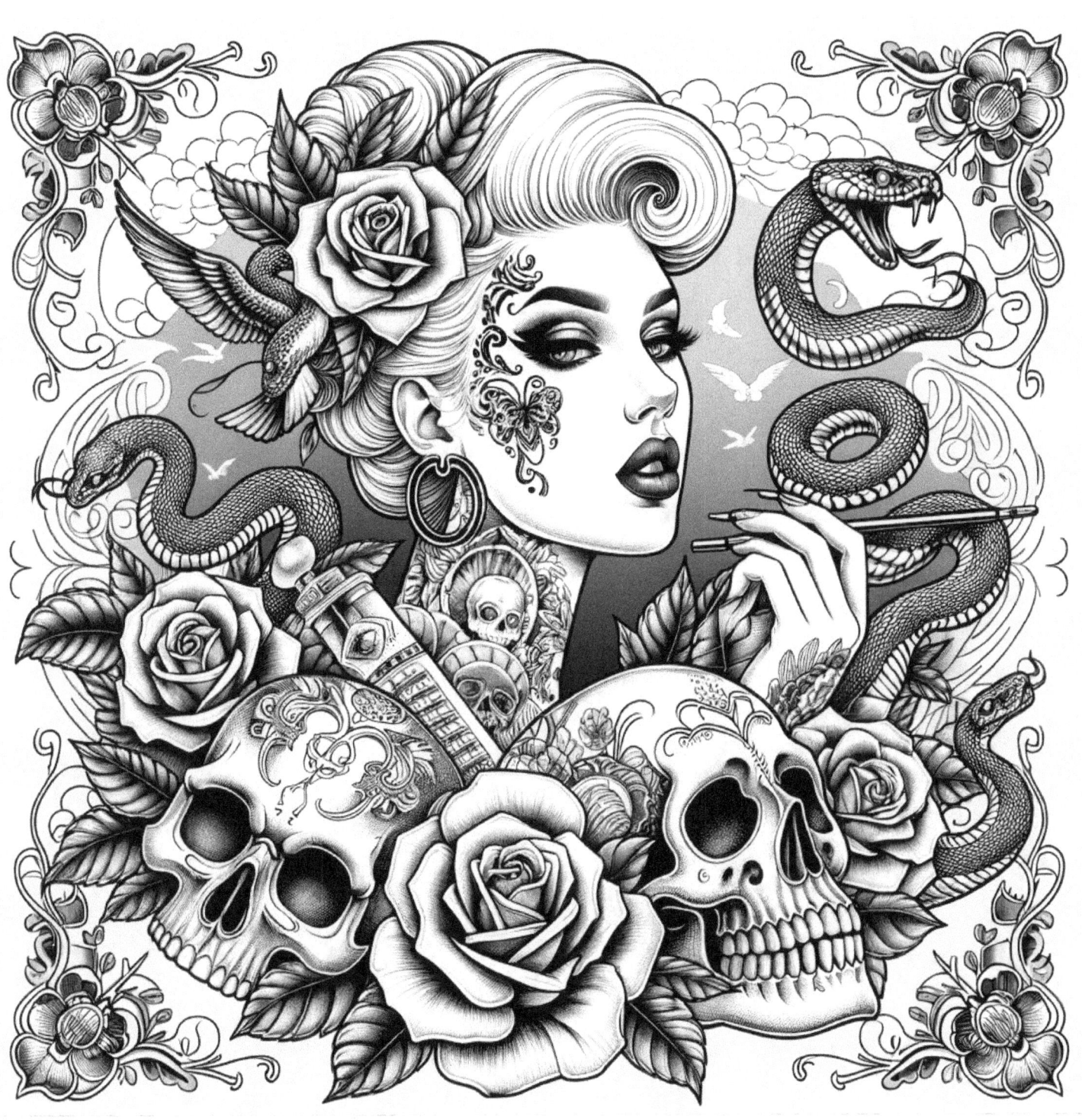

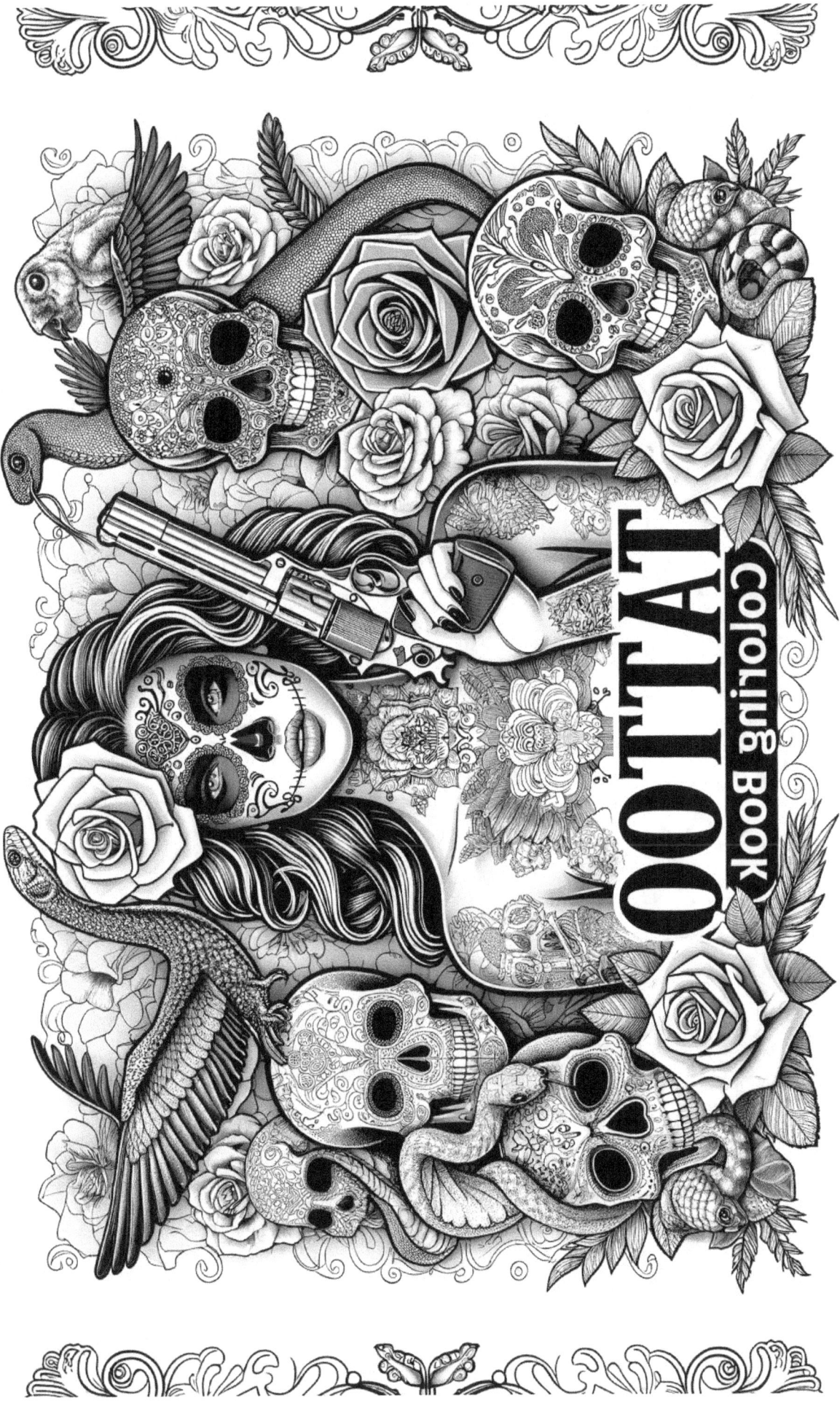

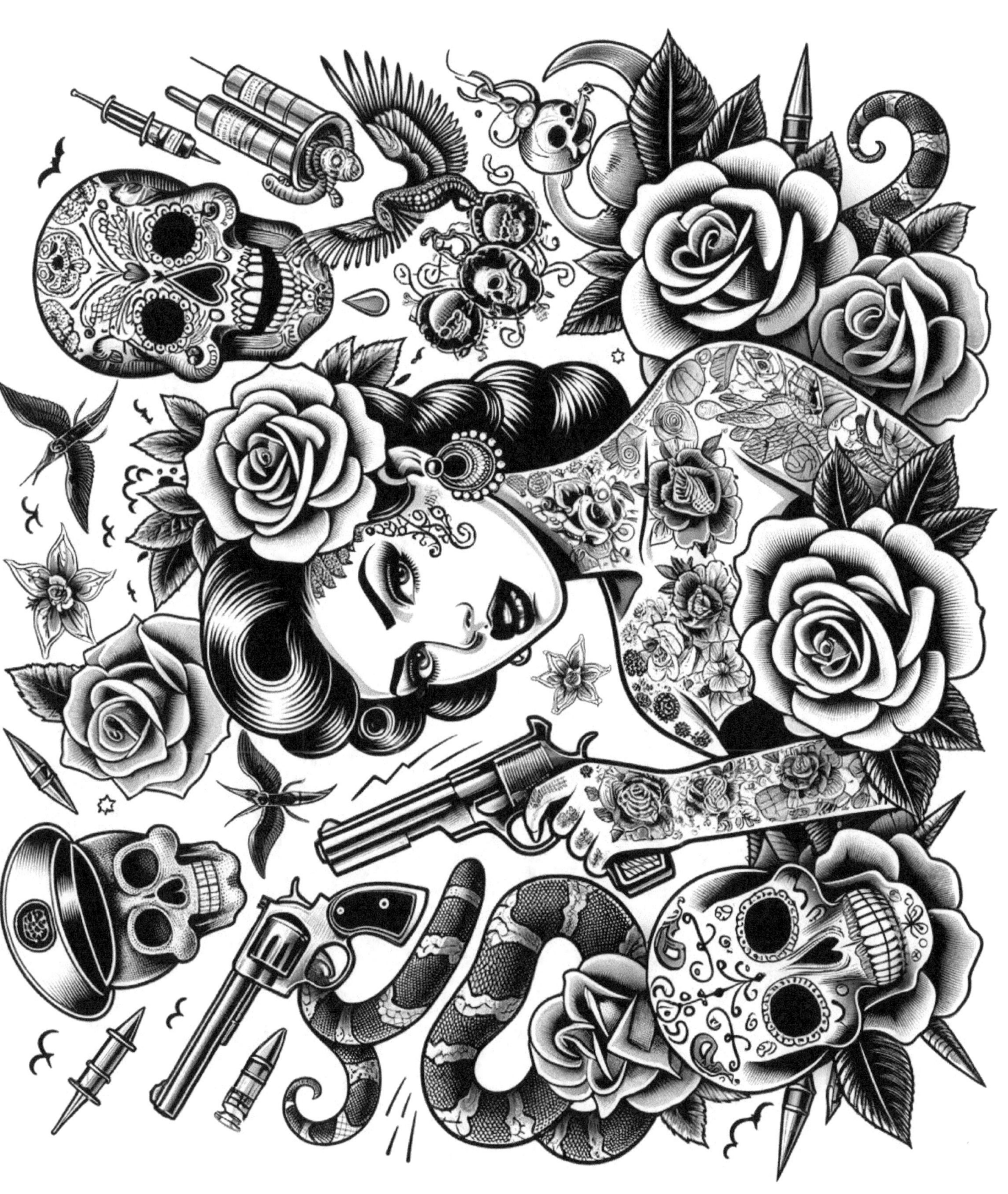

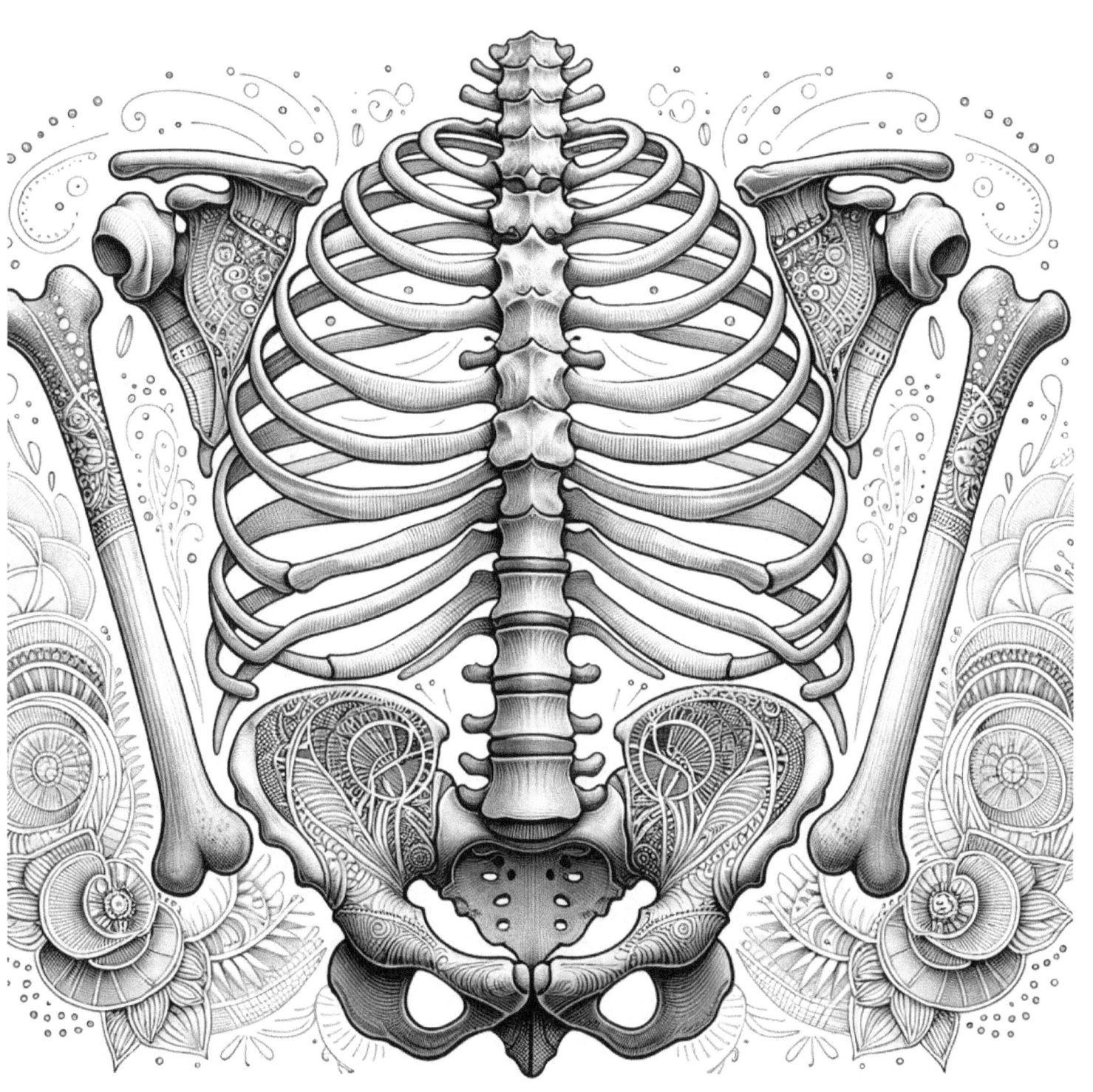

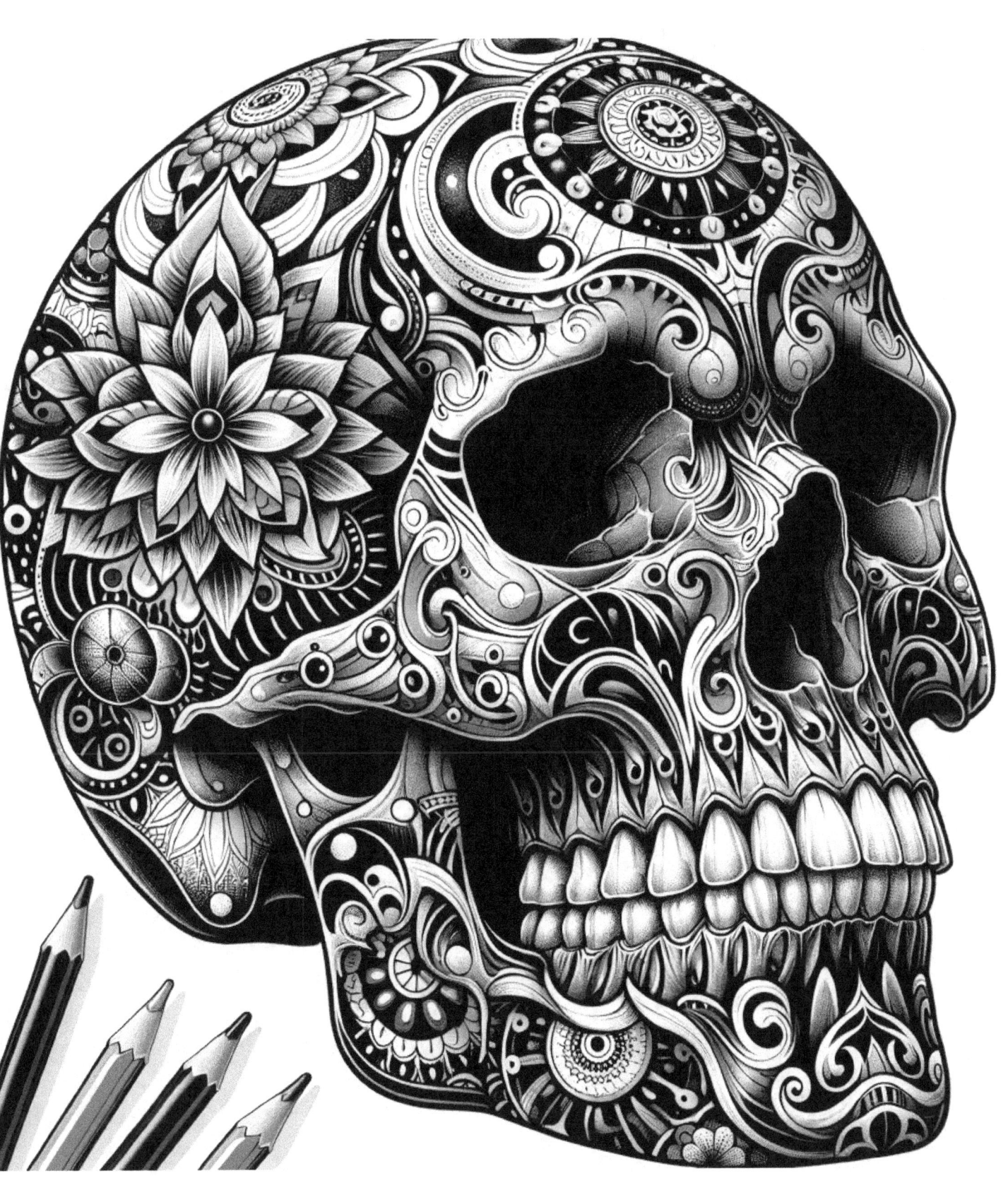

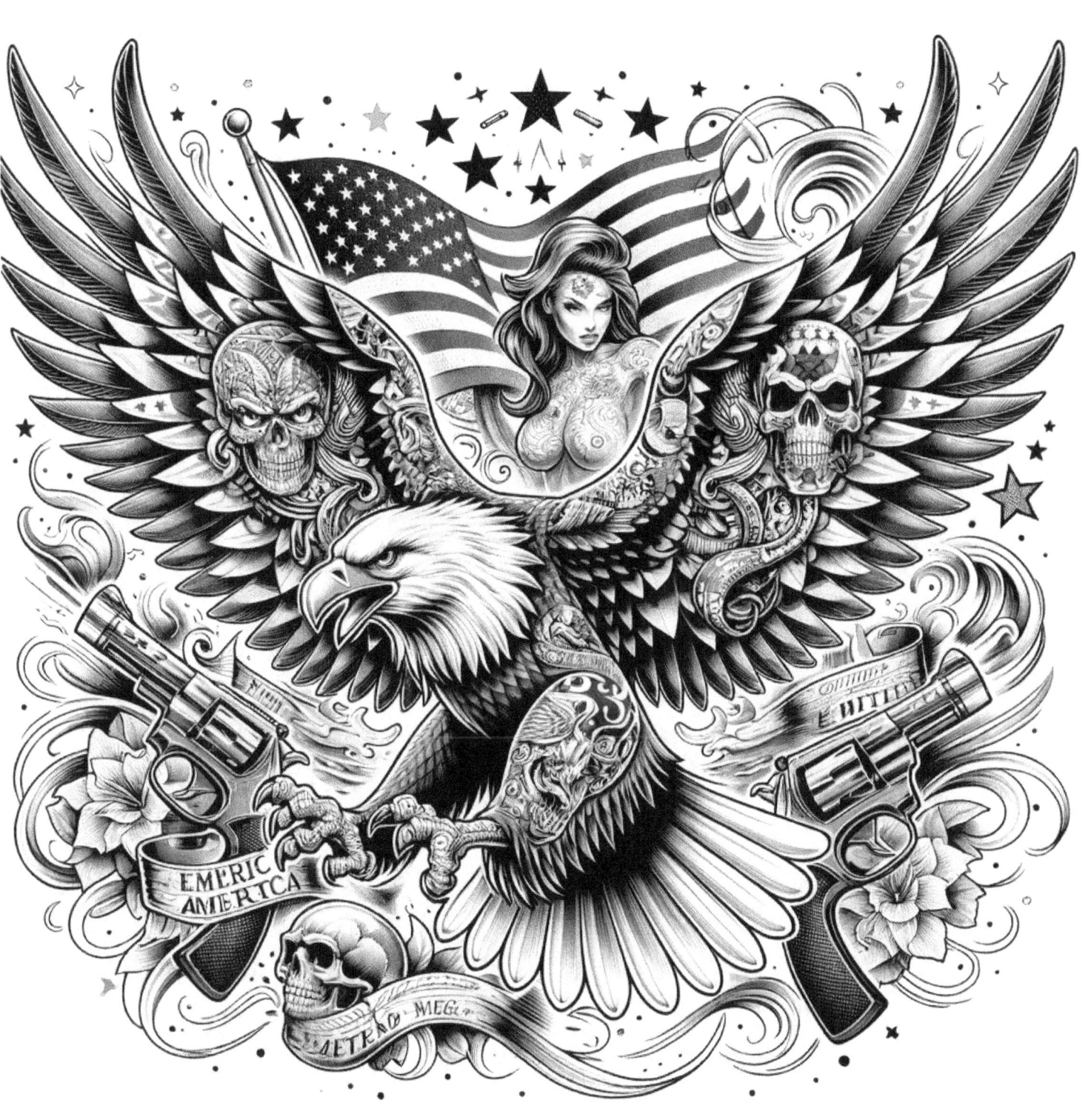

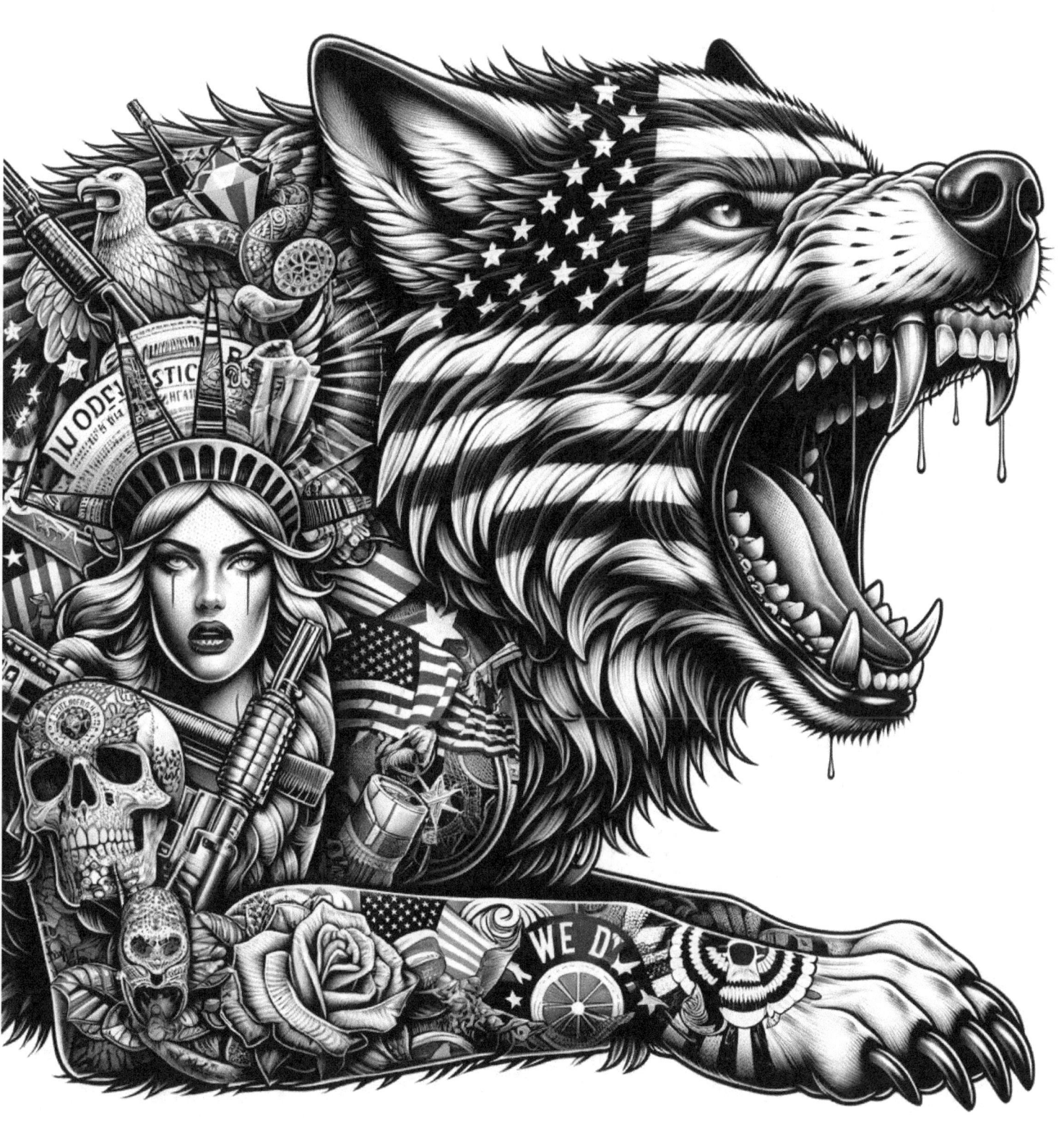

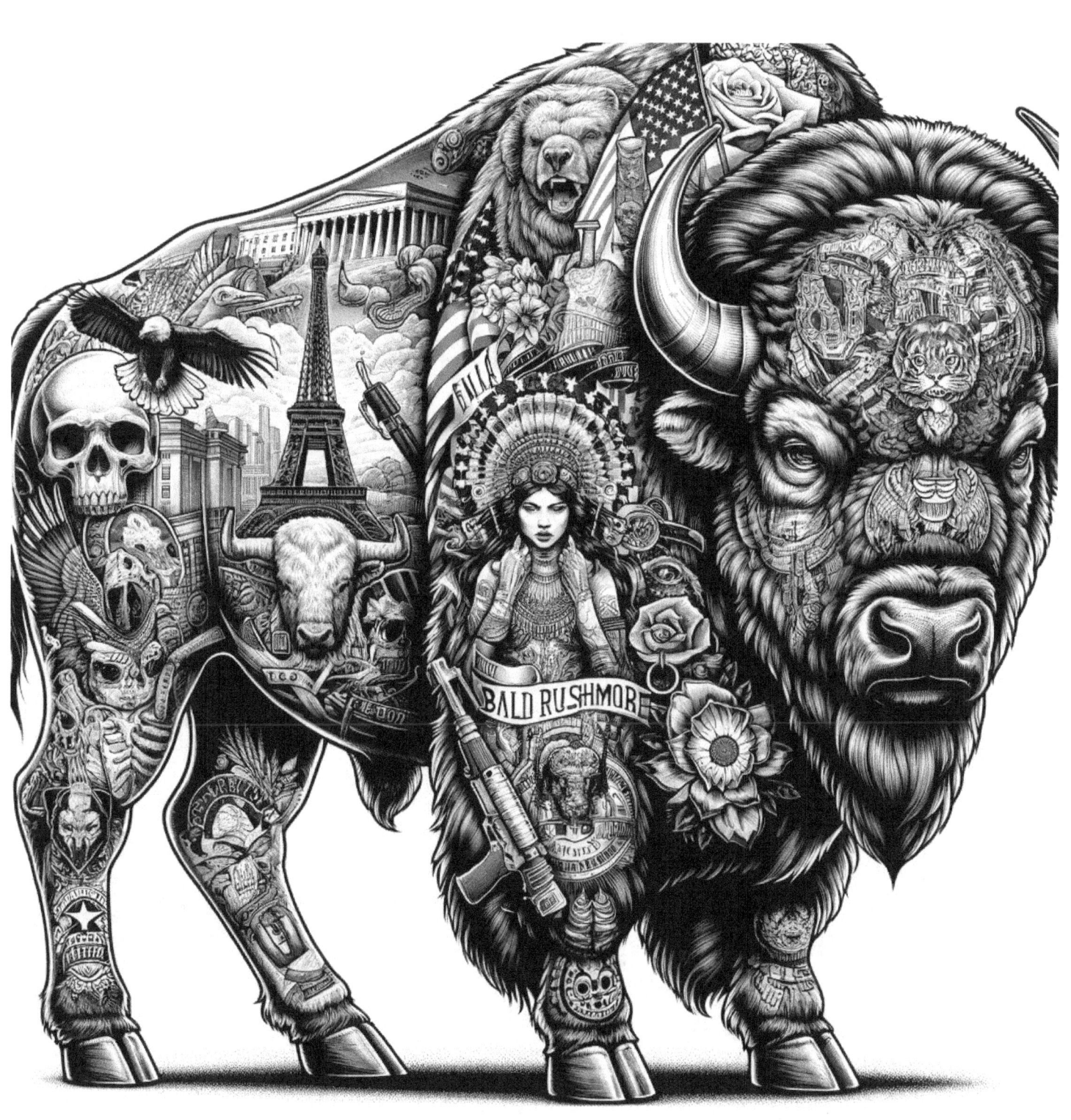

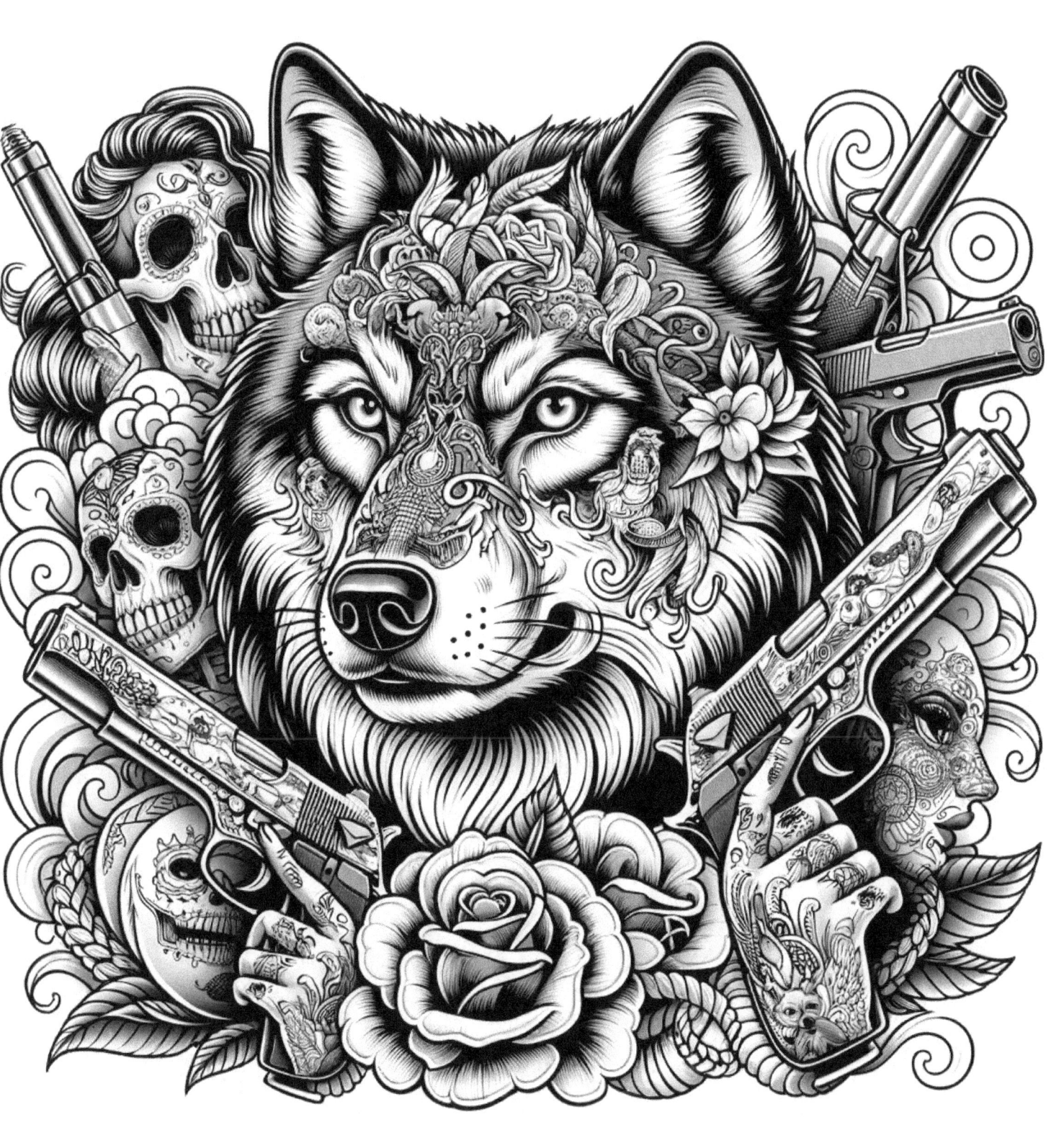

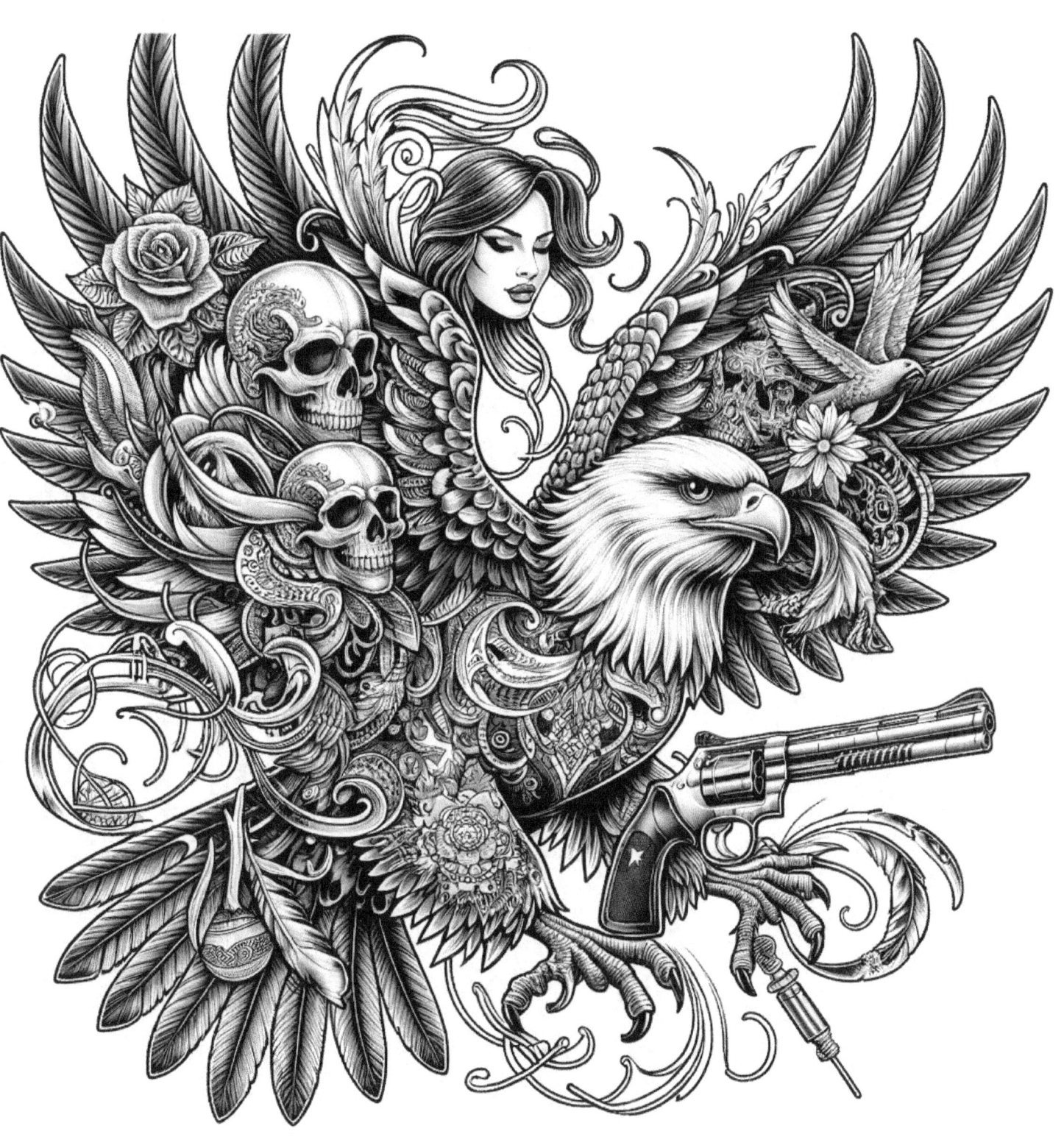

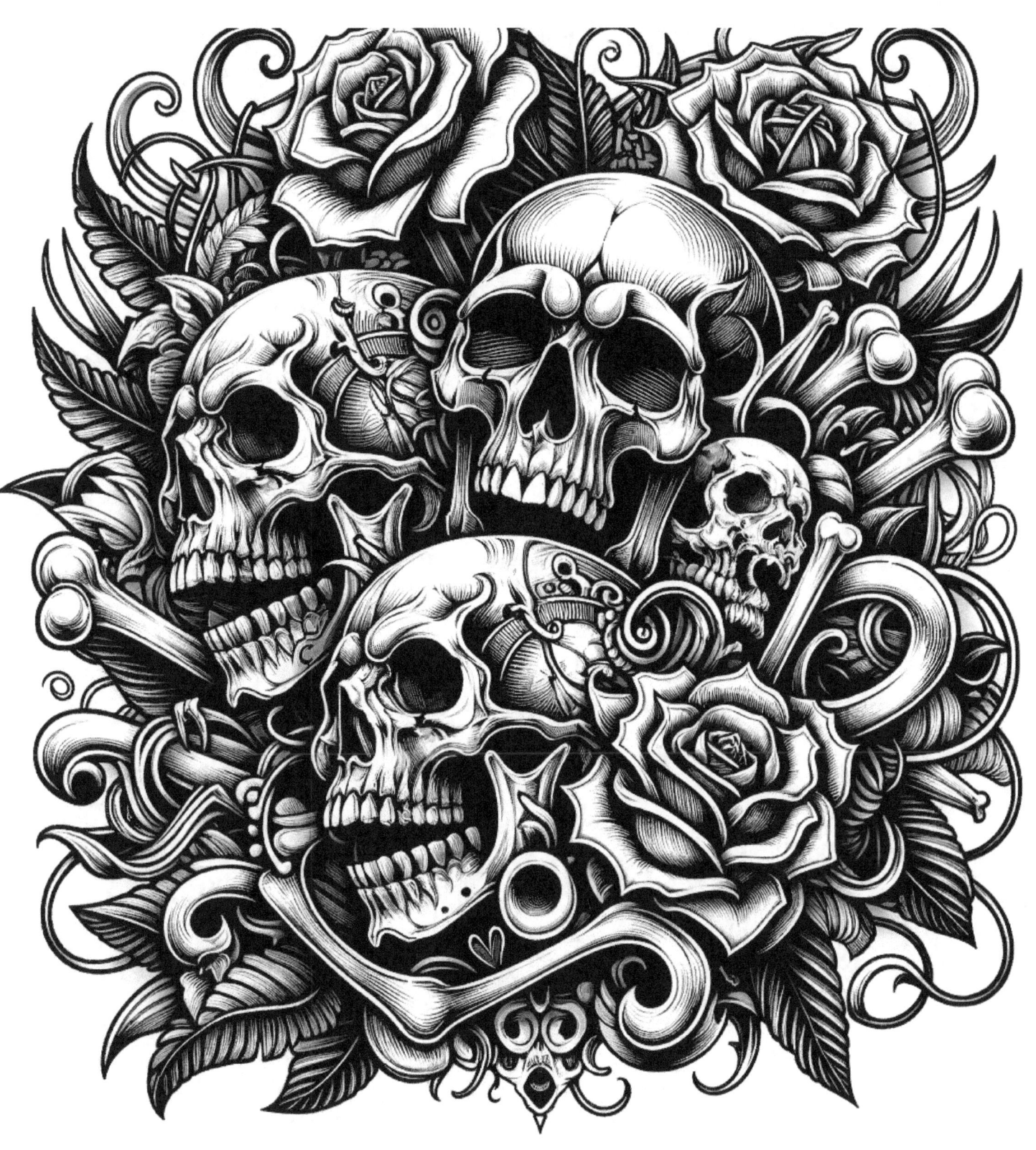

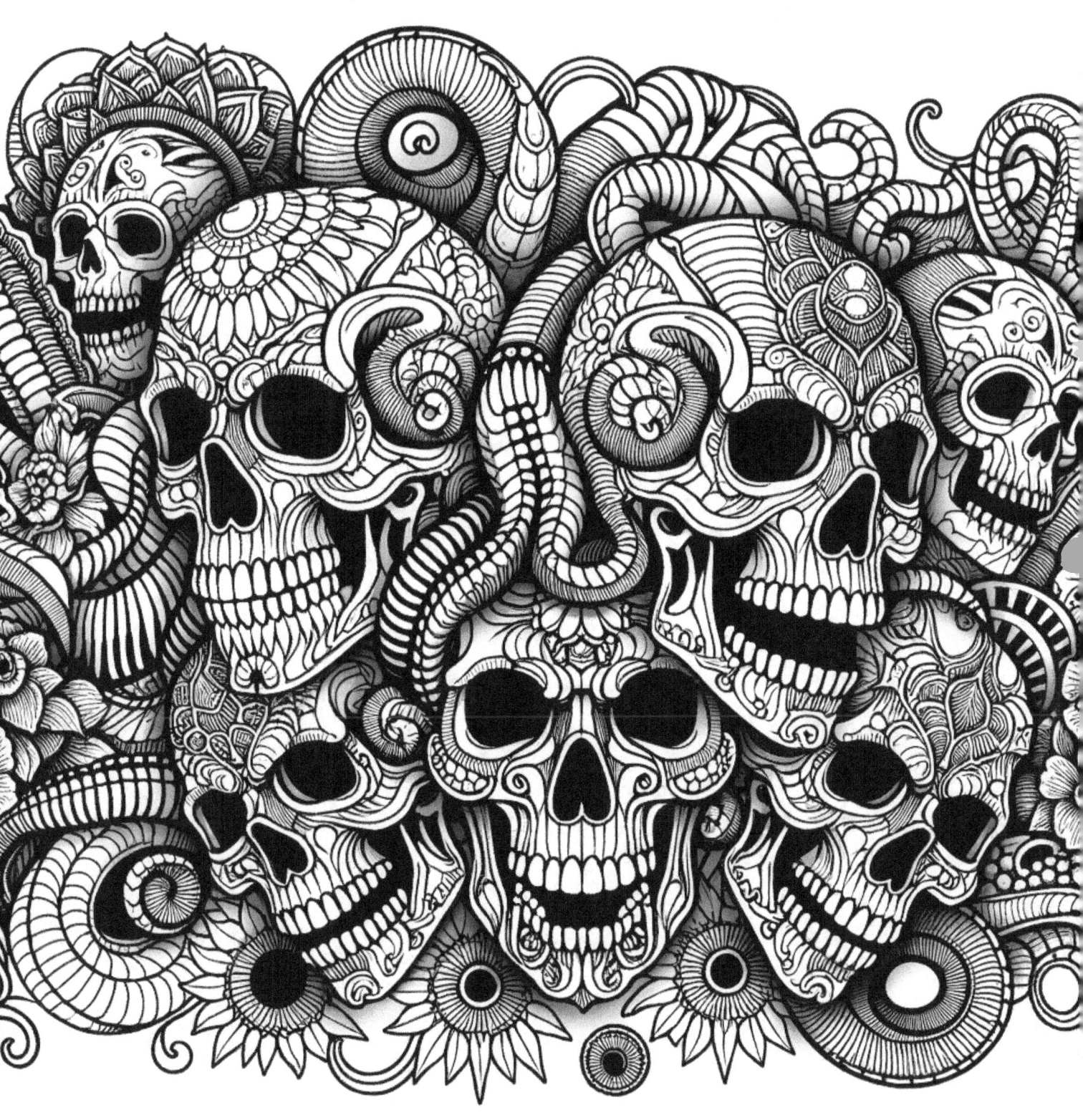

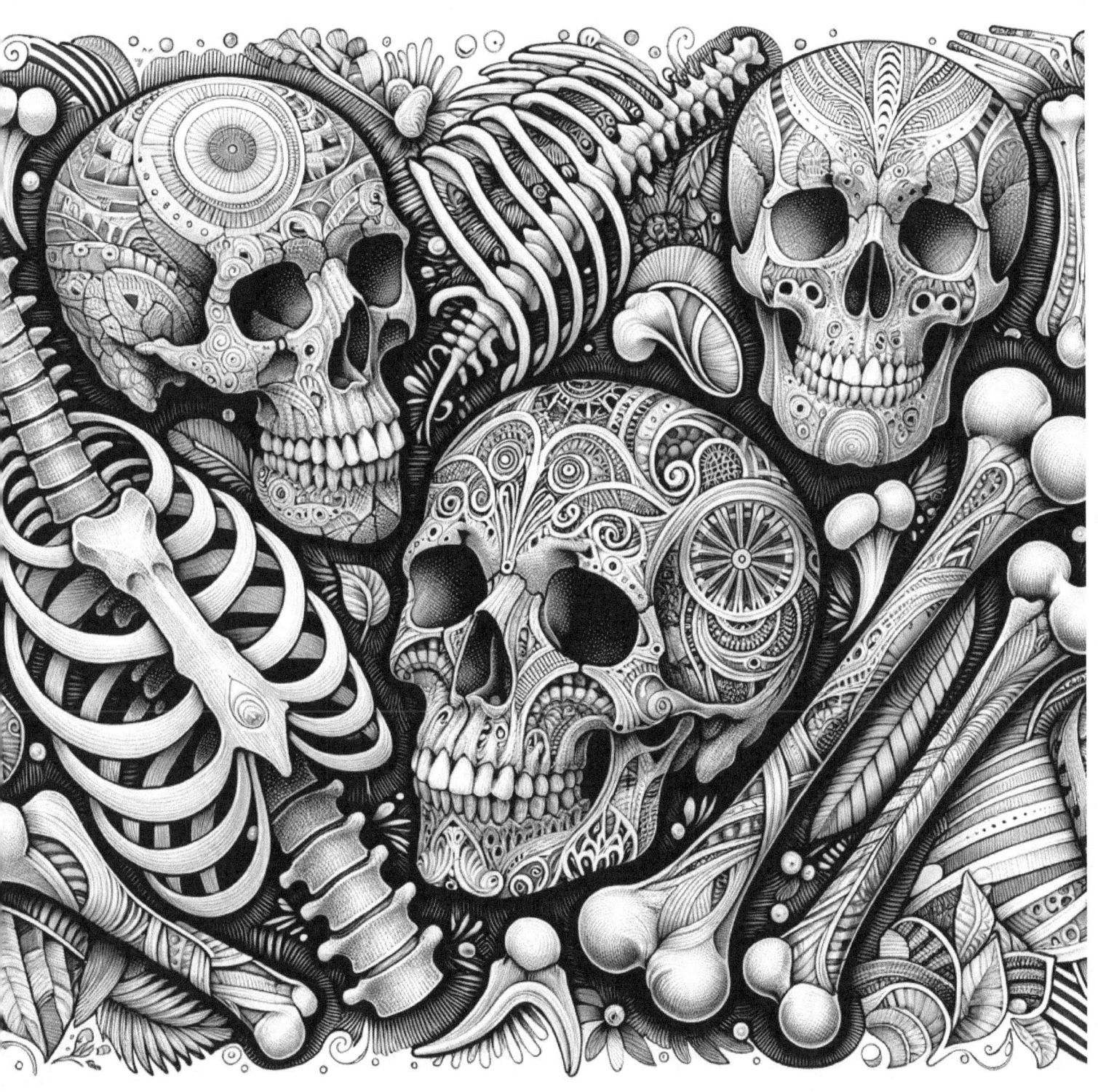

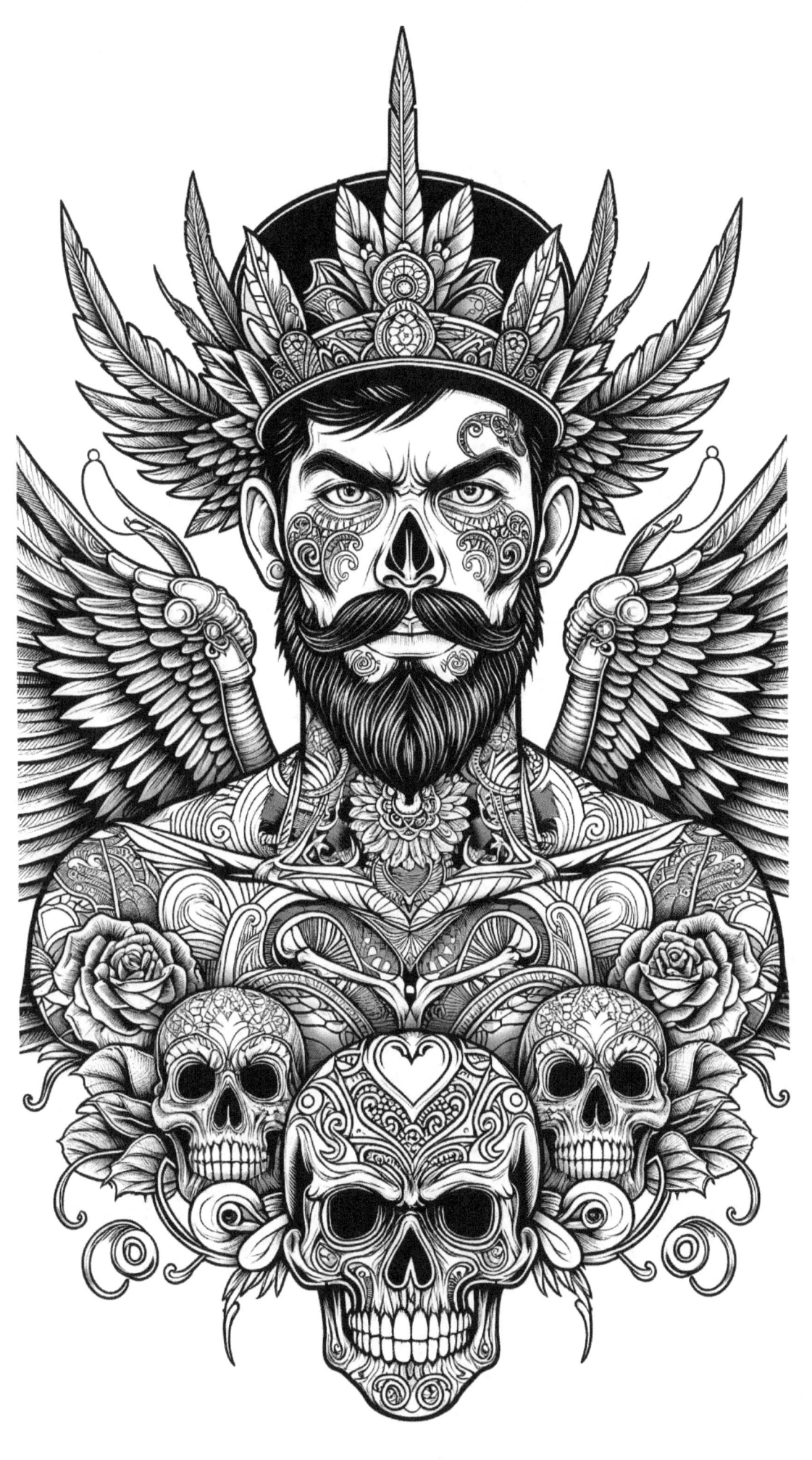

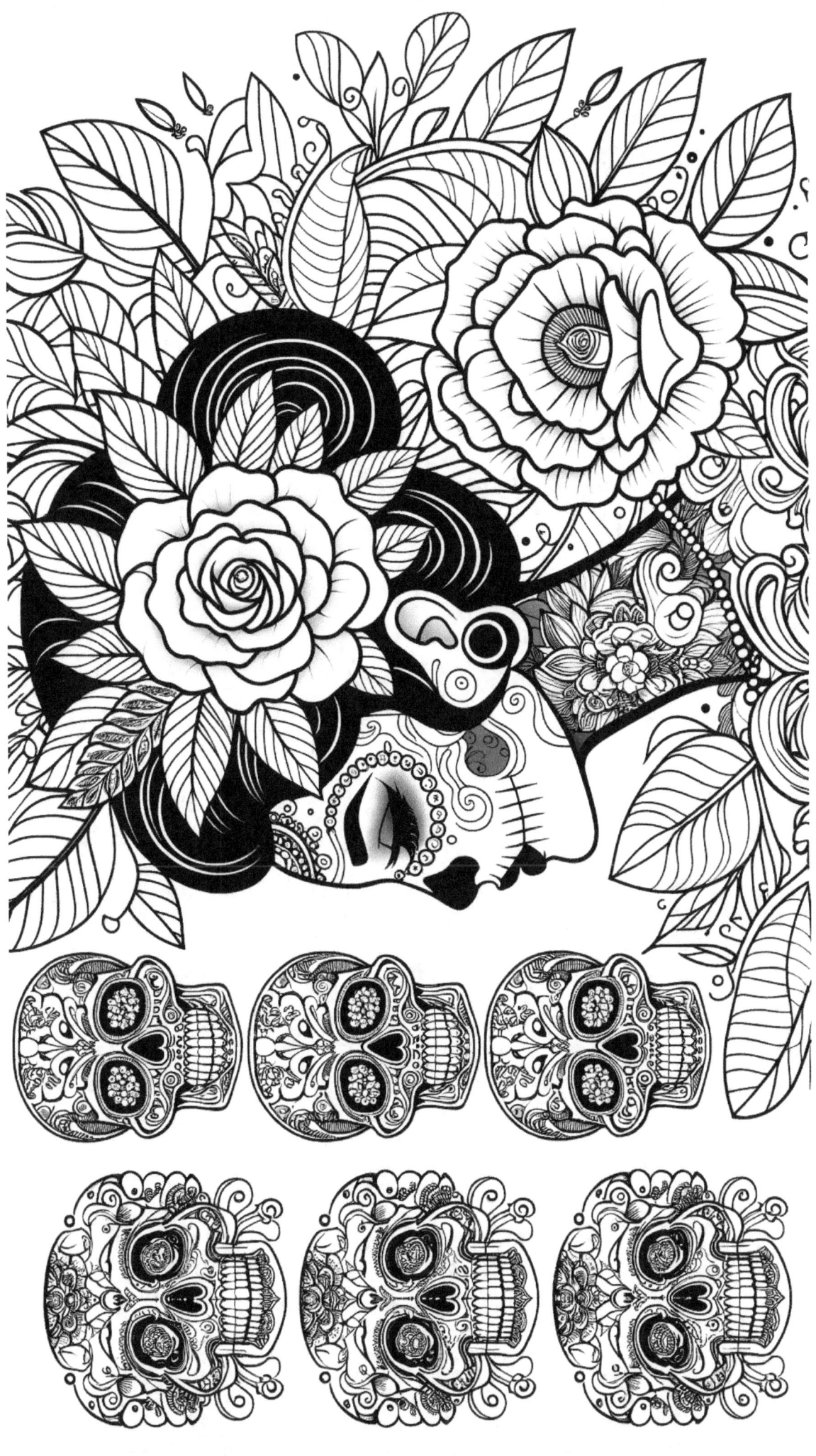

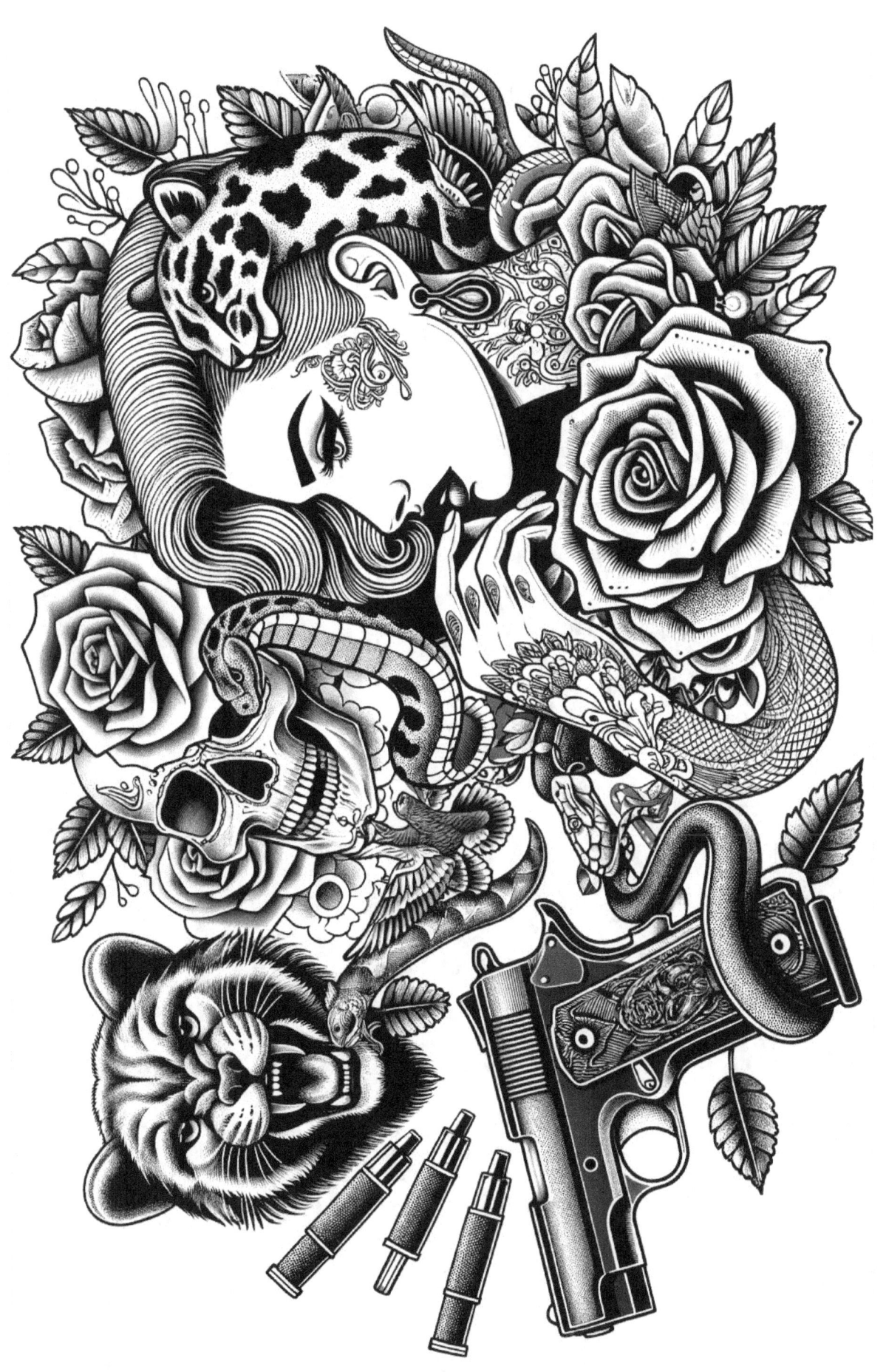

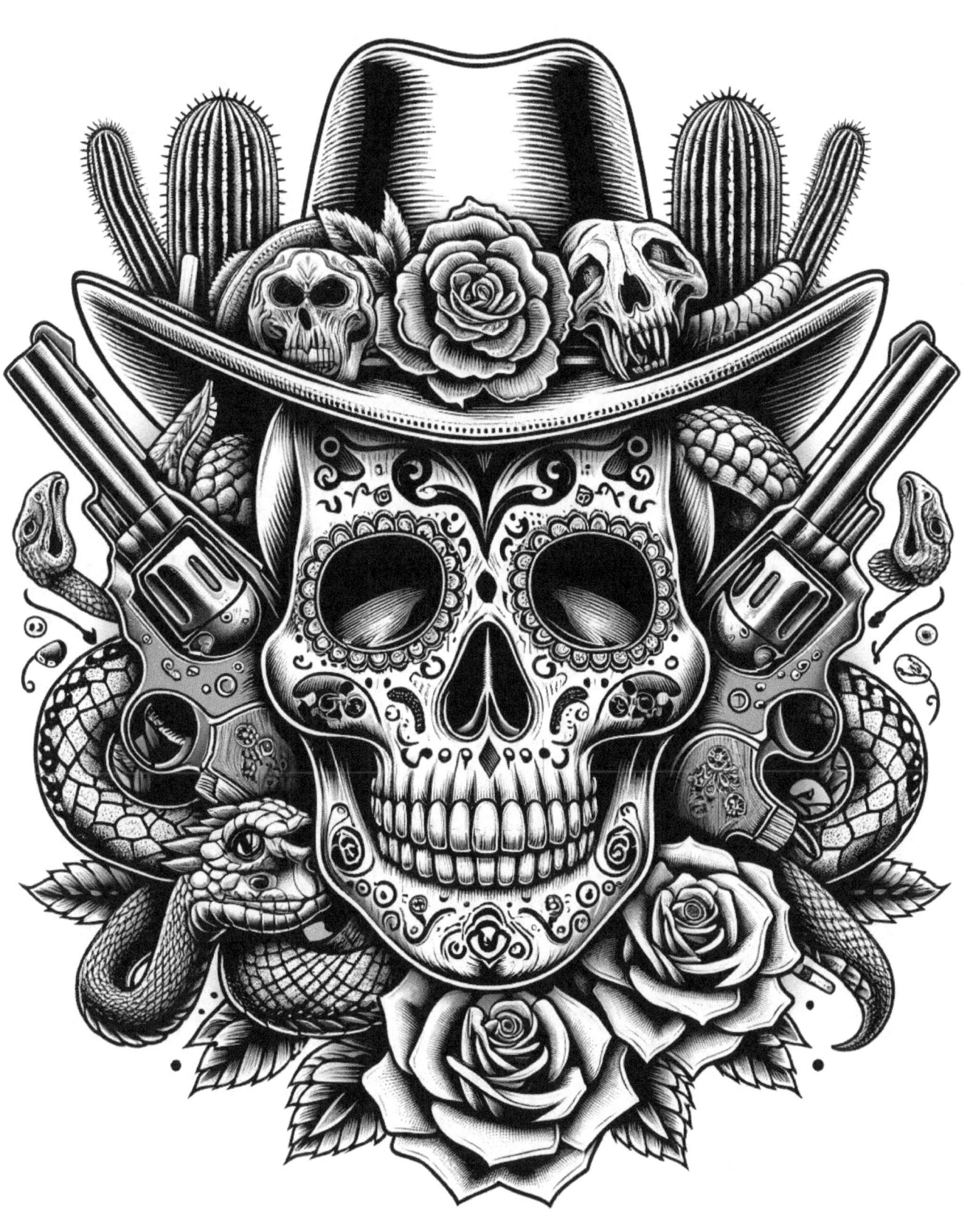

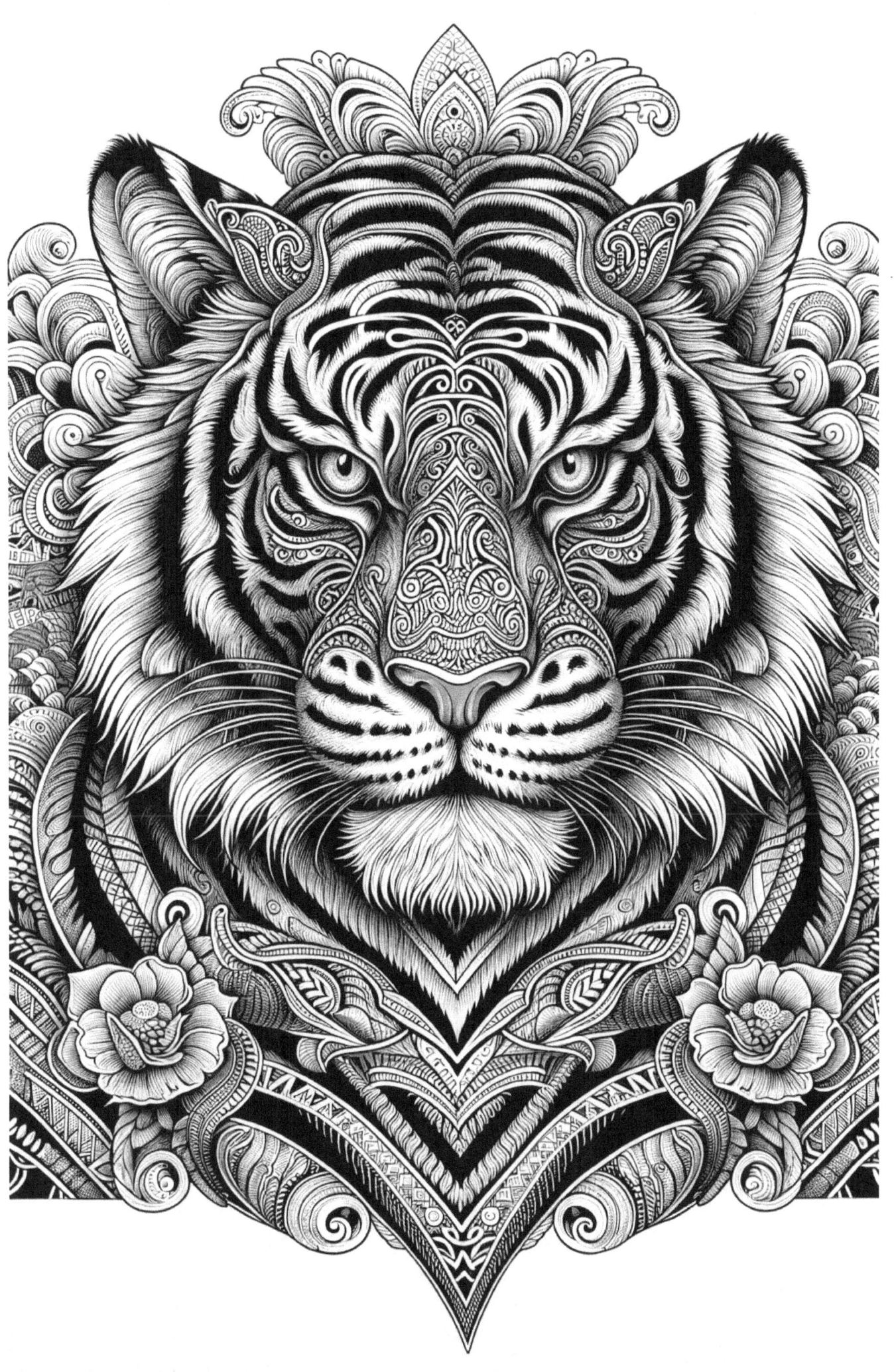

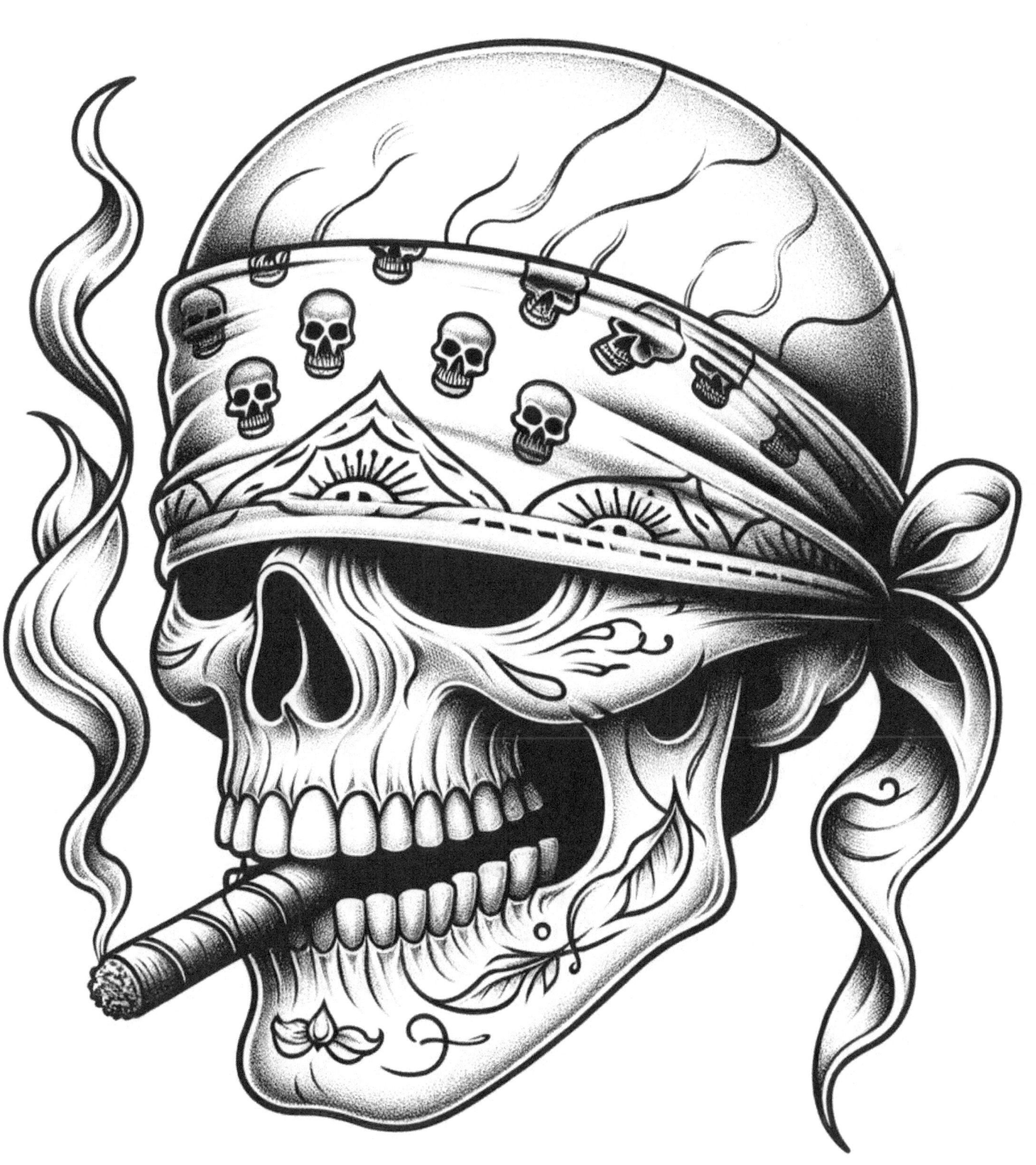

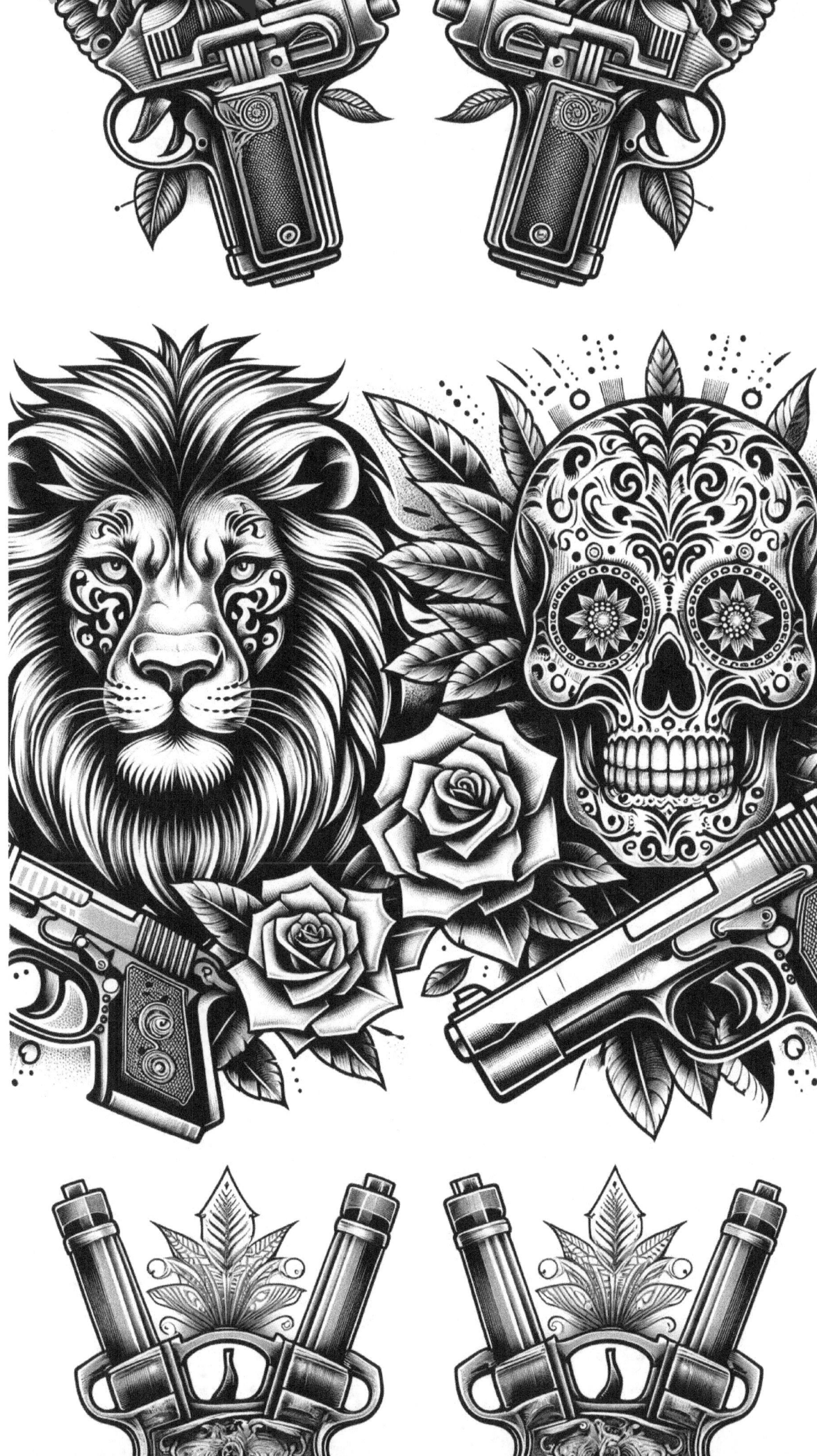

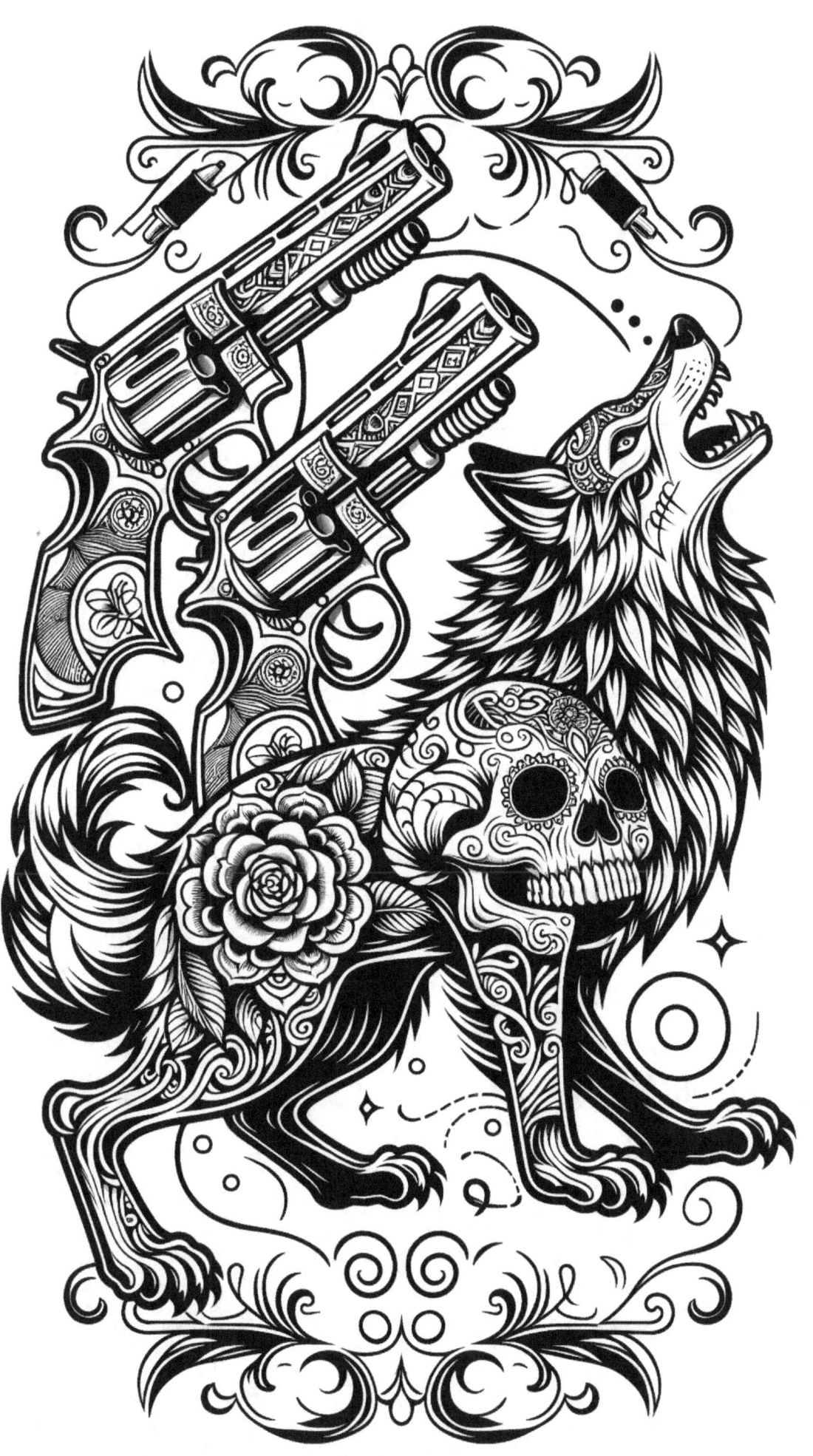

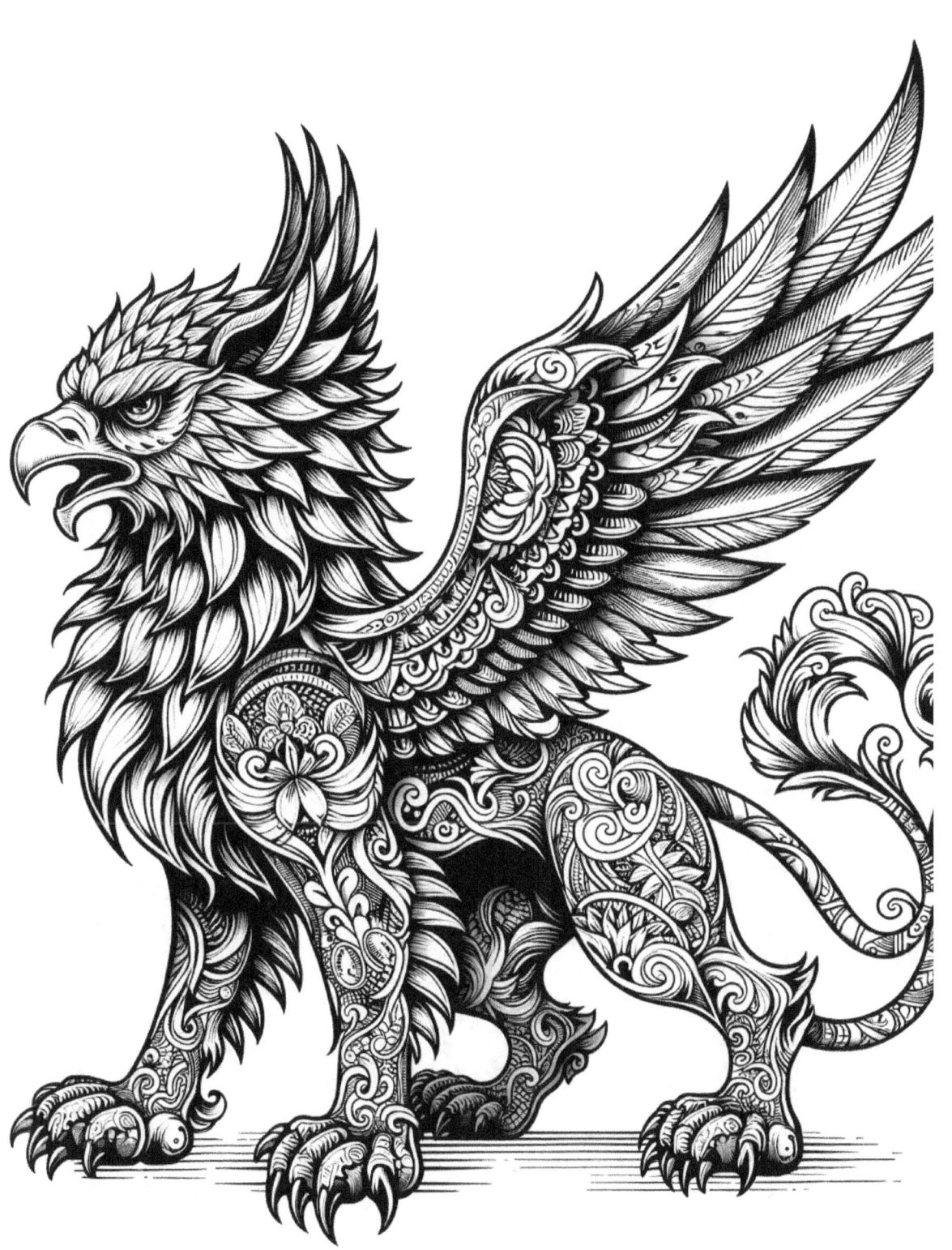

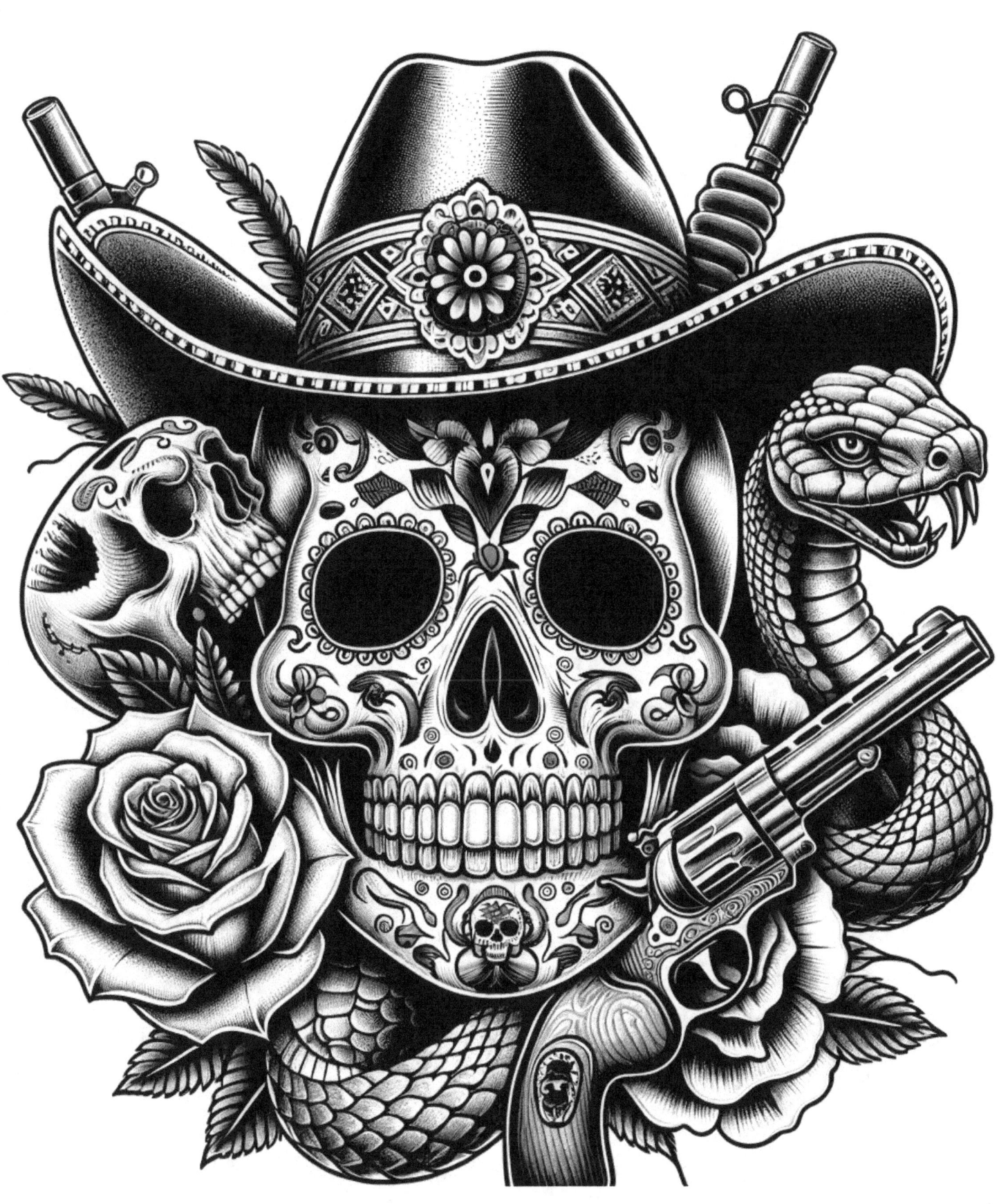

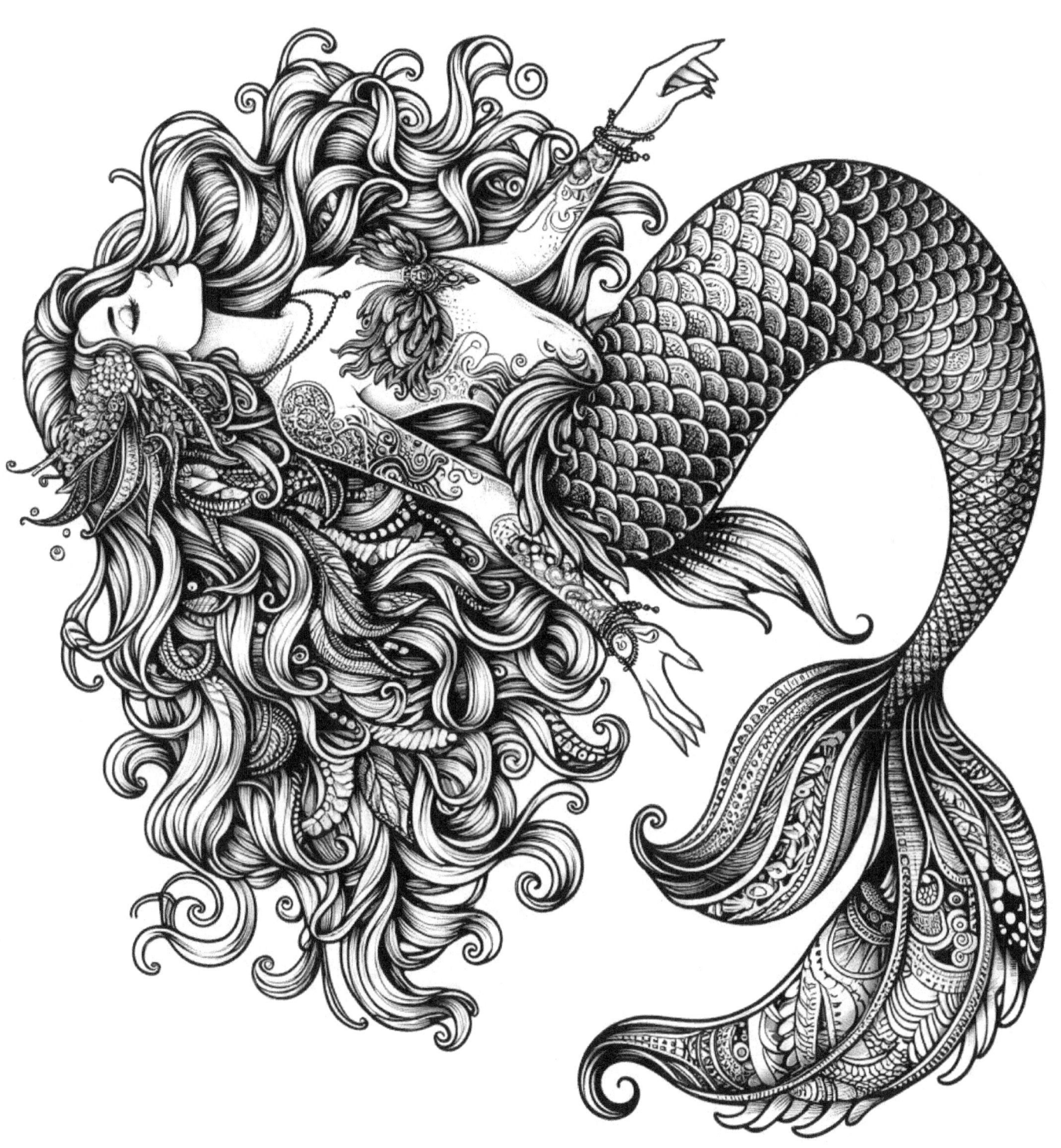

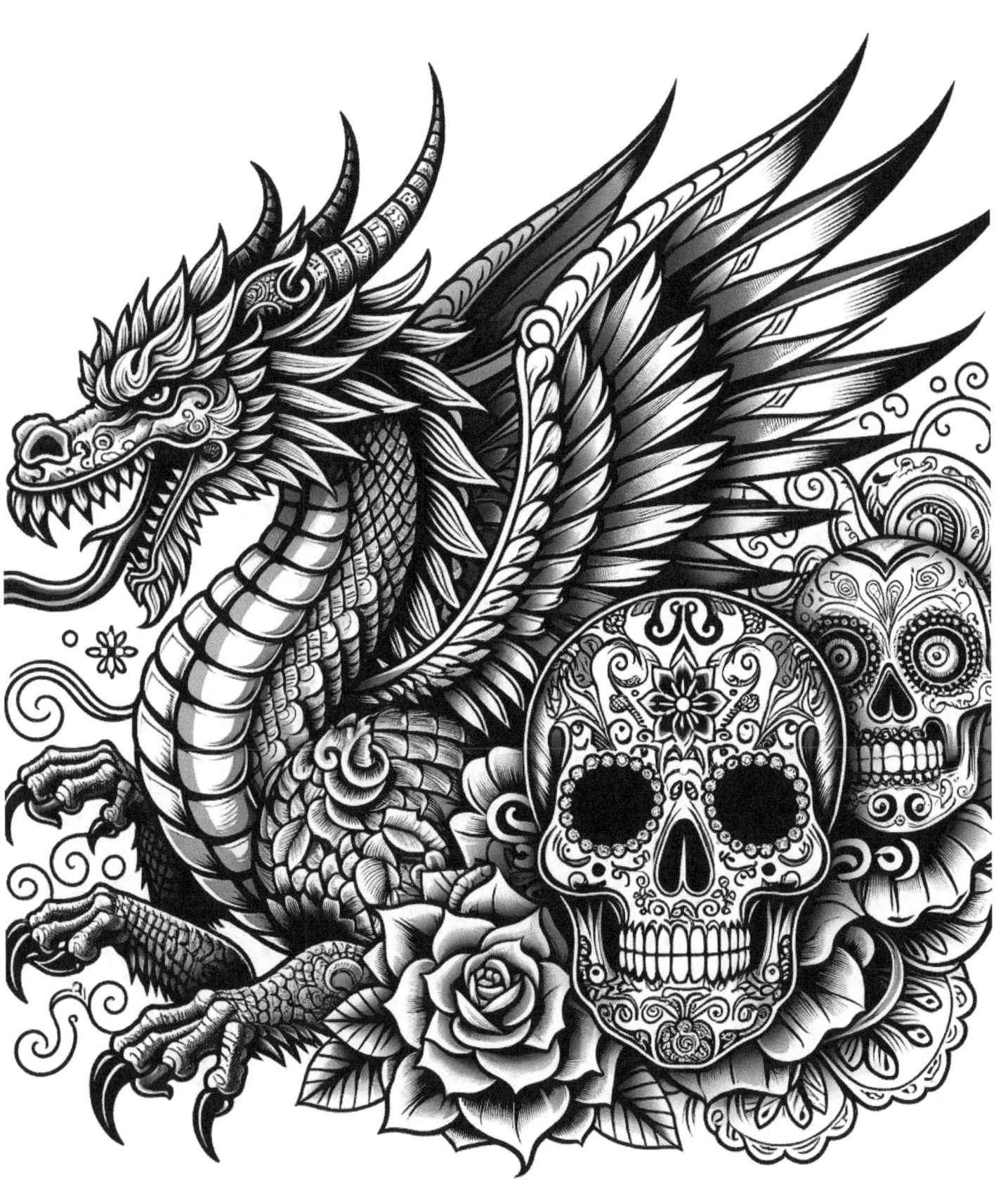

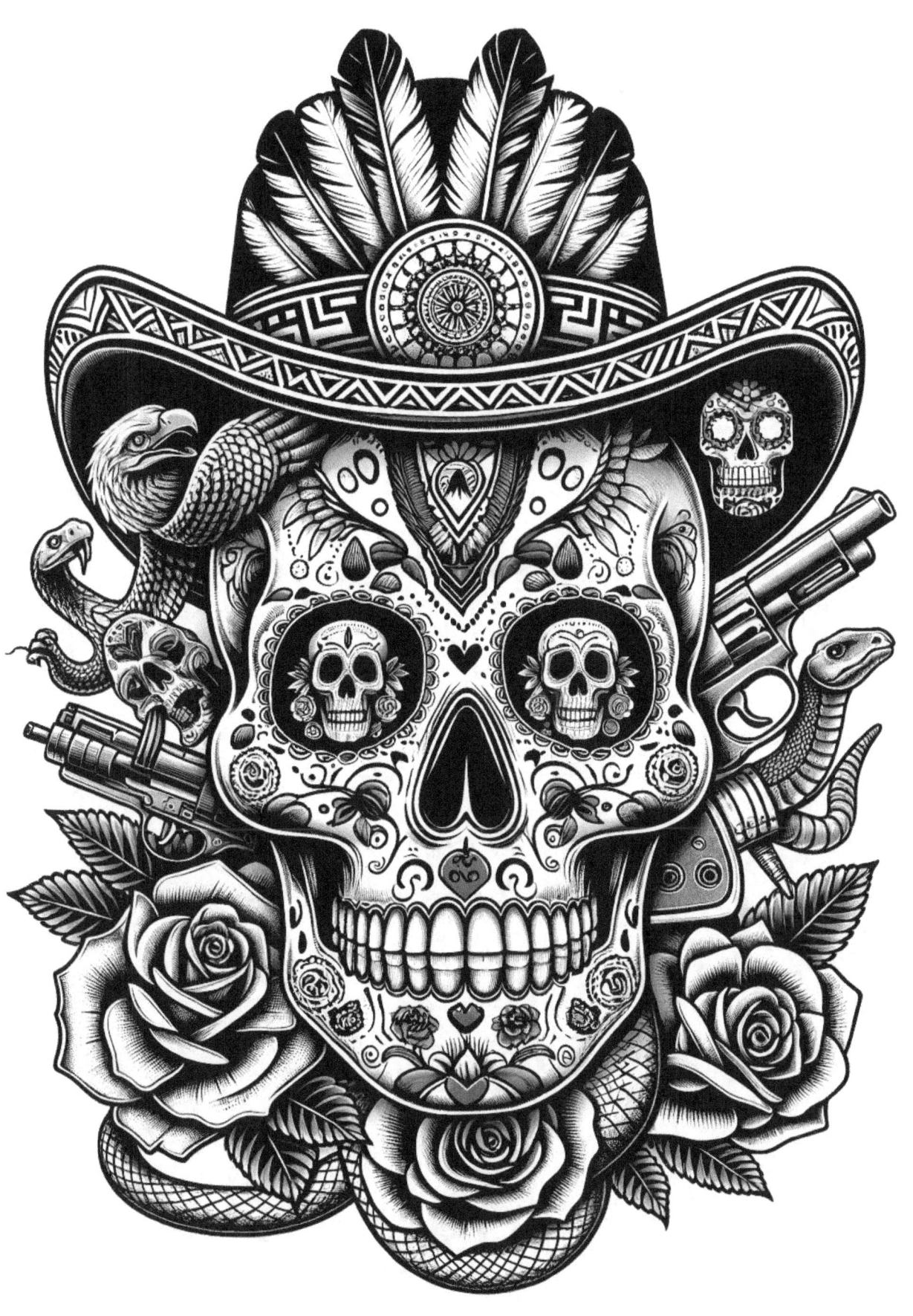

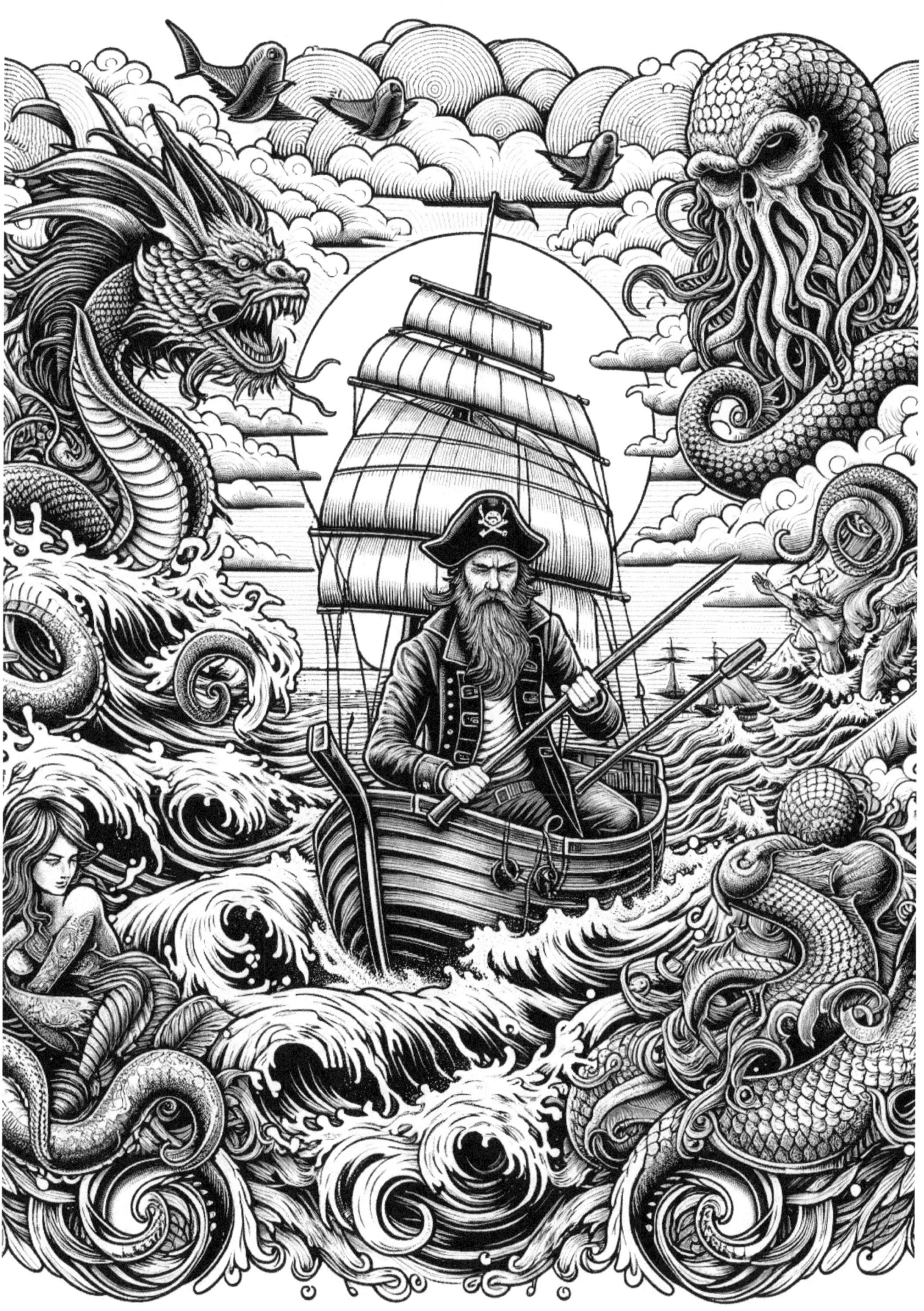

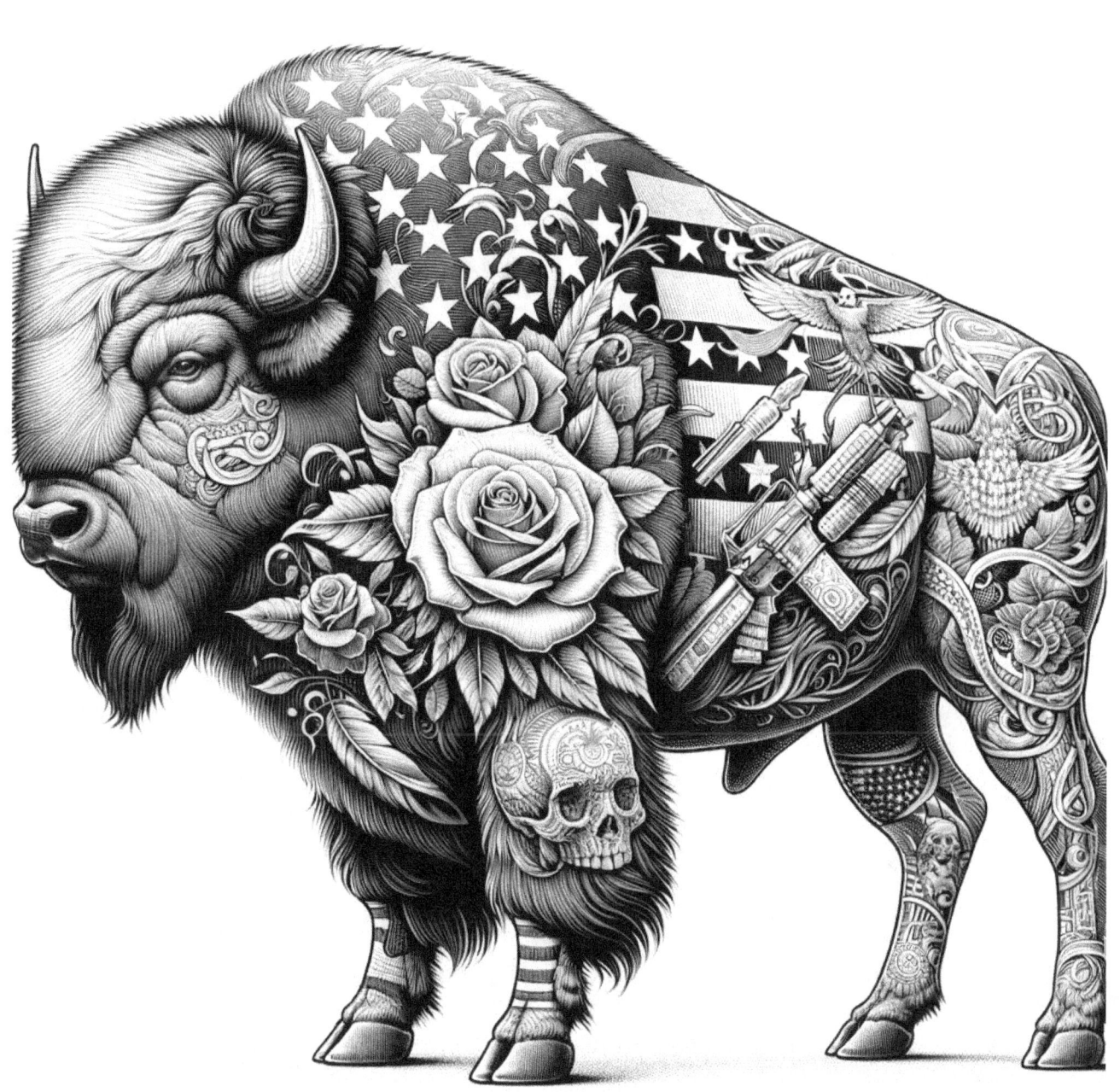

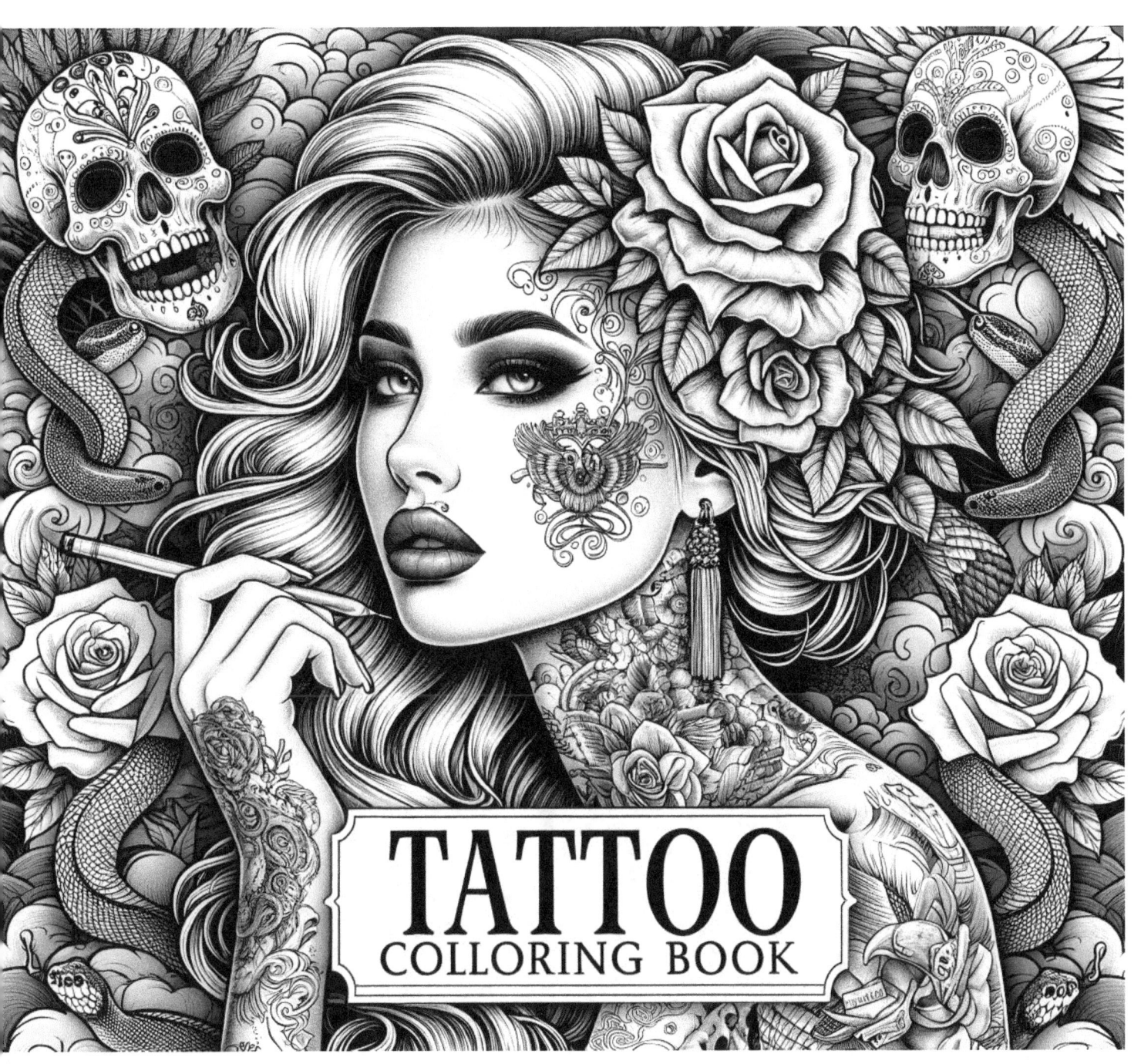

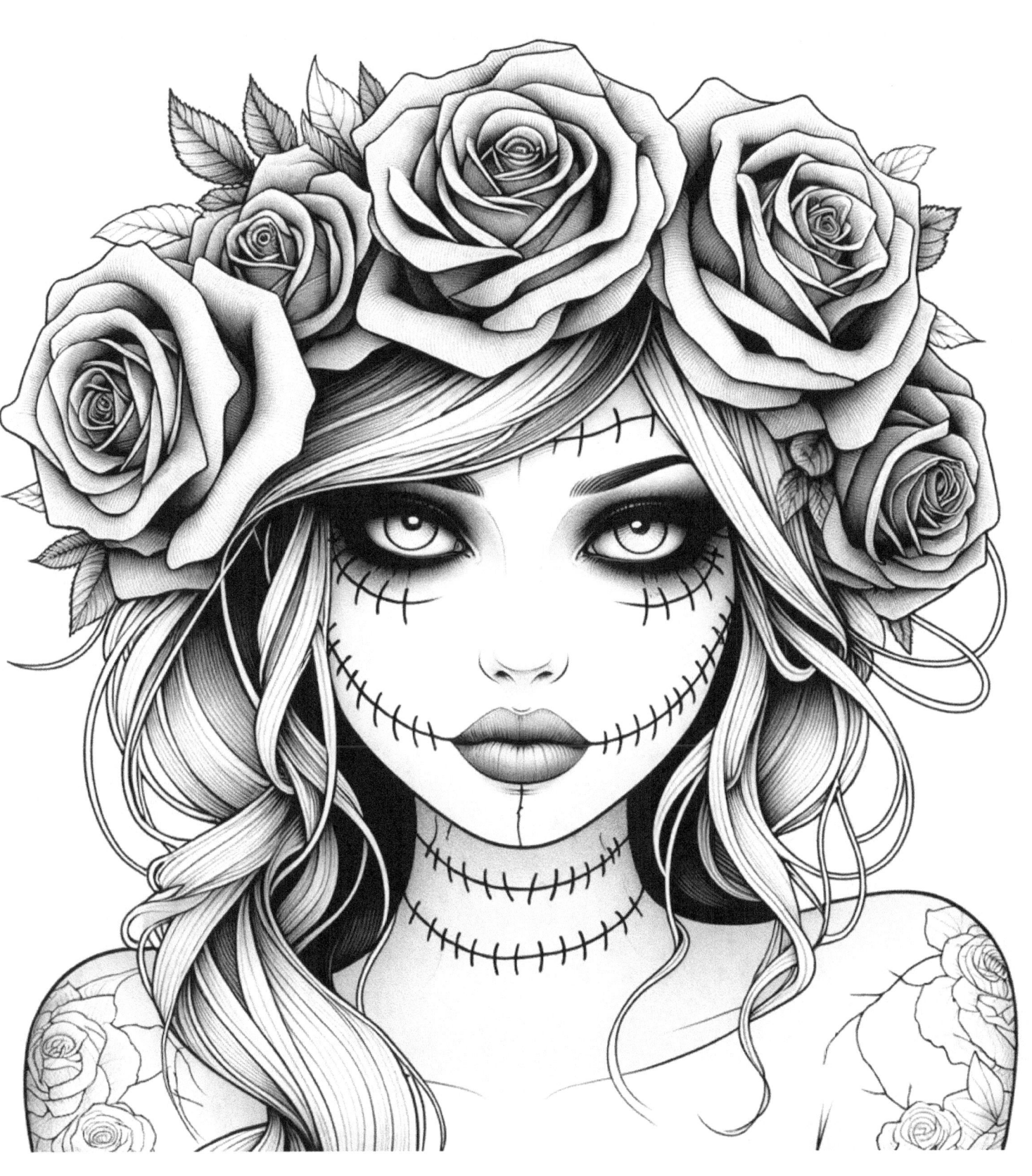

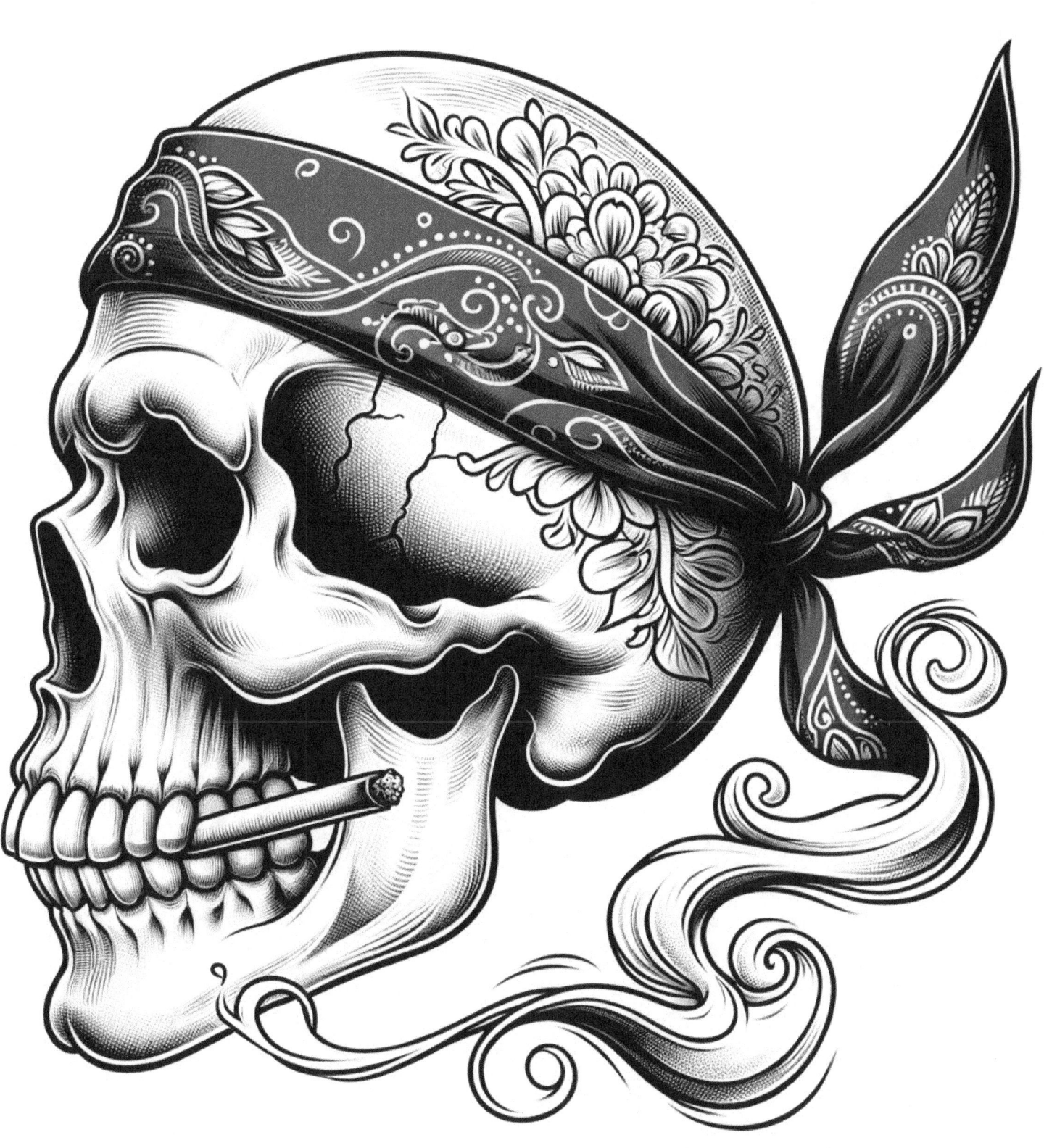

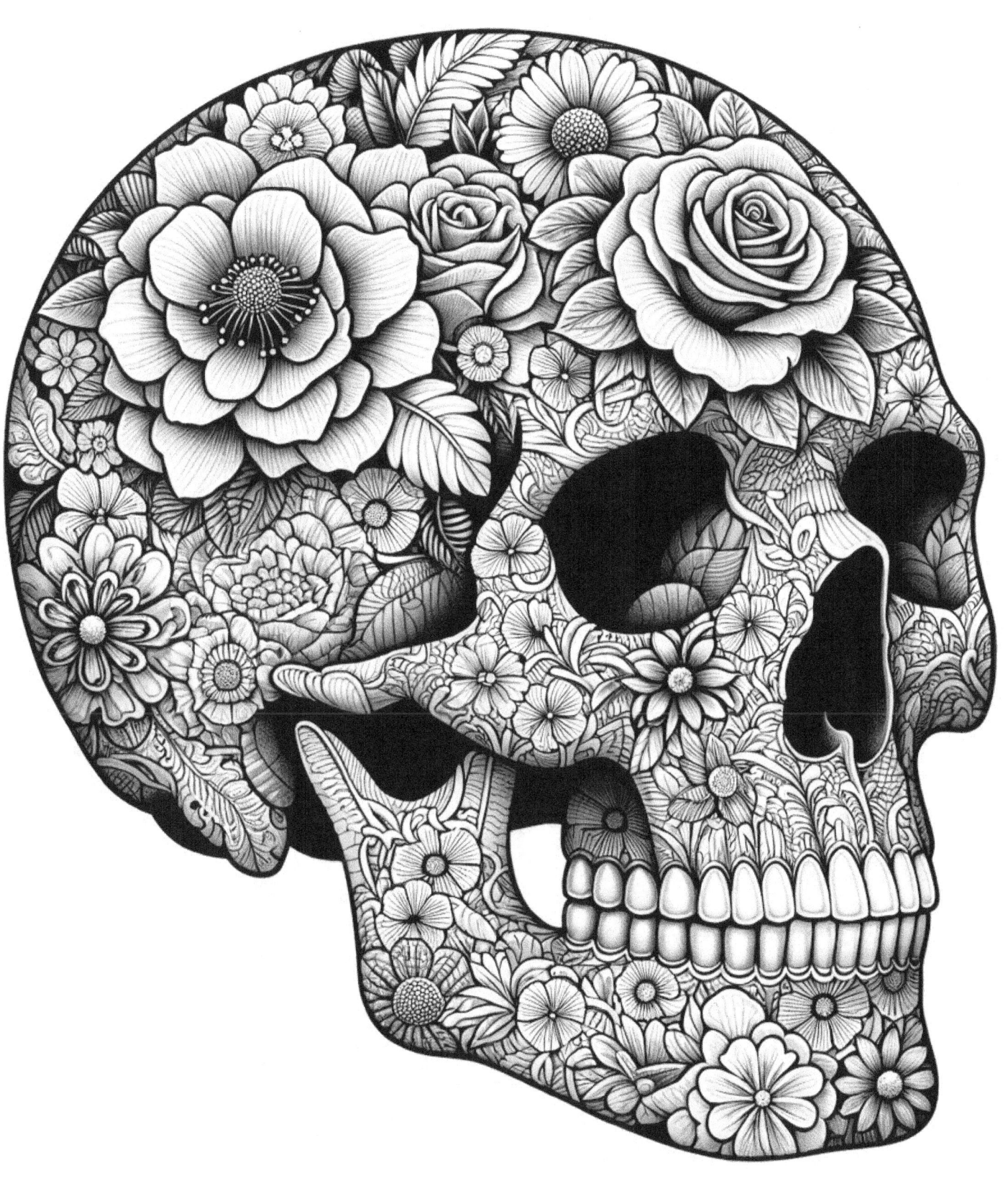

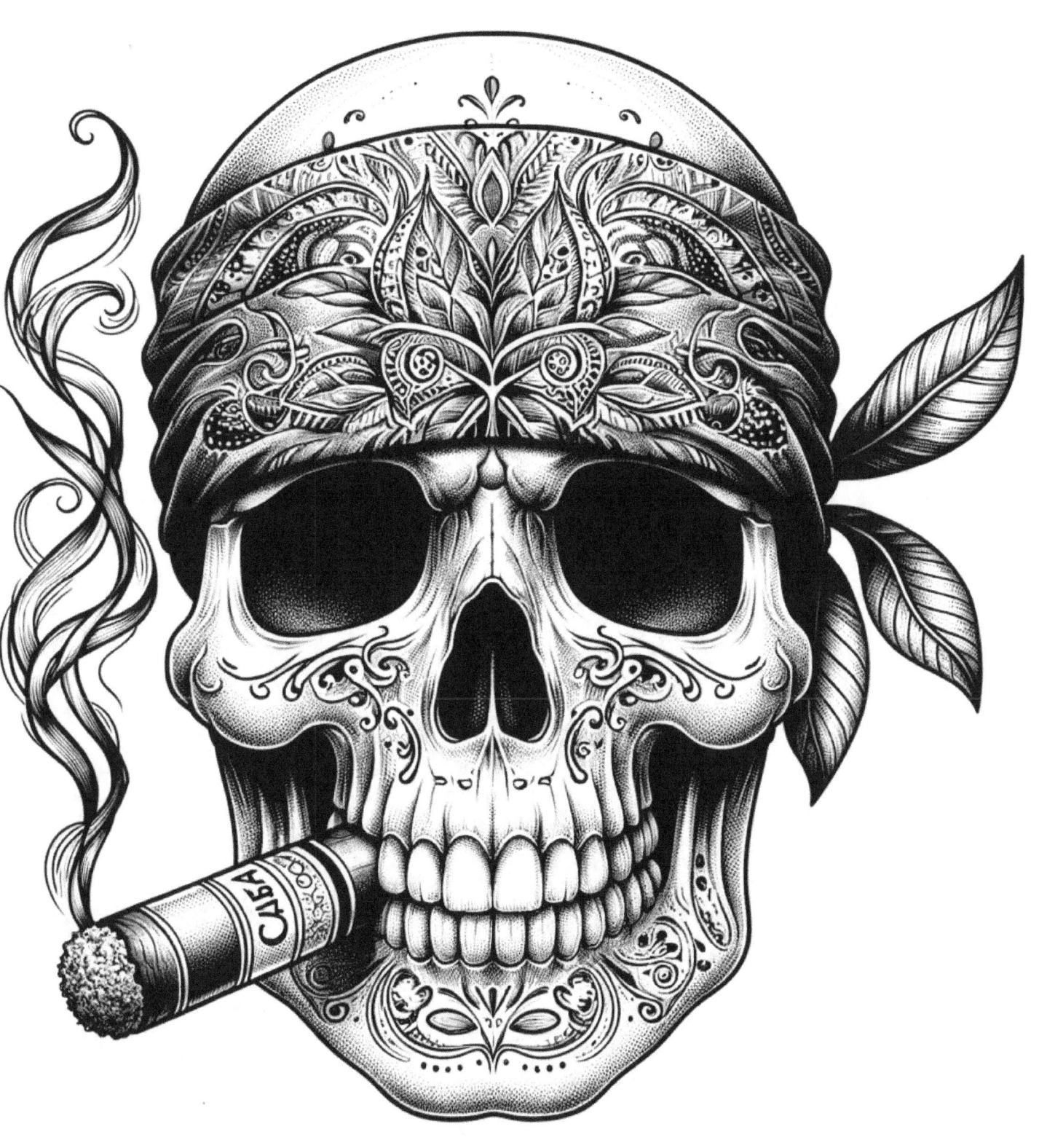

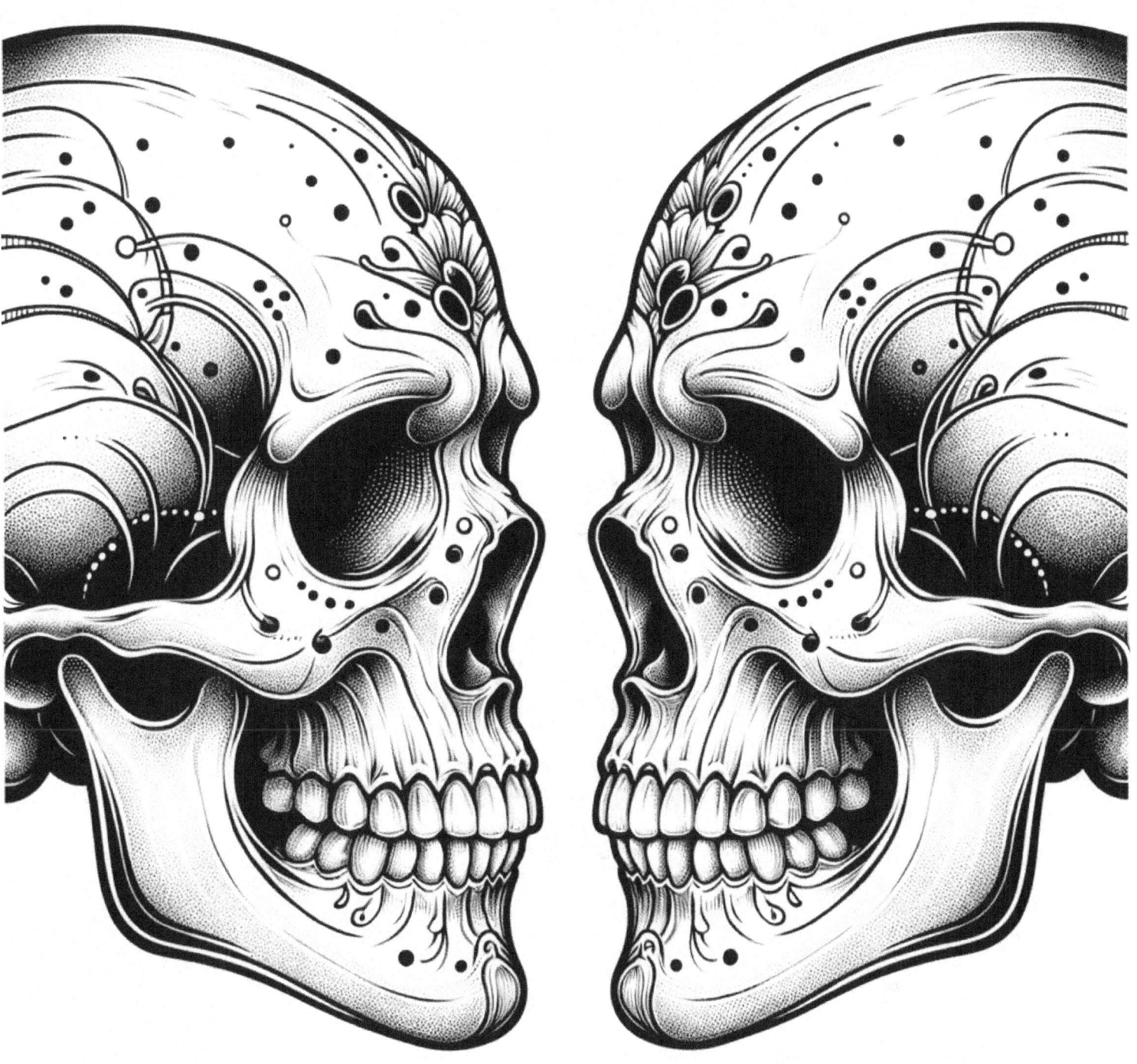

Please take a moment and share your
feedback, opinions, and advice to help me and
my team improve and create better products
and content for you to enjoy in the future.

Thank you in advance!

NOW, Grab your FREE PDF for more Coloring Pages
Use this Link; https://bit.ly/37MjeCw
Or Just Scan The QR Code!

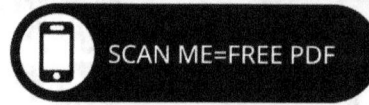

SCAN ME=FREE PDF

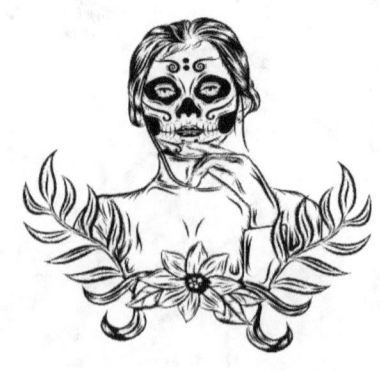

www.ingramcontent.com/pod-product-compliance
Lightning Source LLC
Chambersburg PA
CBHW080104010626
45794CB00014B/3123